How does one become a poet? As Cindy Lee Scott begins, "Looking back, what an incredible life I've had! It is most definitely overwhelming when reflecting on all the magnificent, as well as difficult, times I've been through. Yet, here I am still embracing life, fighting my battles, and growing in this never and ever-ending story of me. Dramas and comedies, sadness and elations, melancholy and exuberance, failures and victories, all forming the person I've become."

This anthology of the work of Mountain Quest Poet Laureate Cindy Lee Scott includes personal stories written by the poet herself as well as objective thoughts added by Professor Dr. Alex Bennet, the Director of the Mountain Quest Institute, a research and retreat center situated in the Allegheny Mountains of West Virginia. As you will discover, although these two authors met just a few years ago and have only spent one week together, there is a special connection between the two, which provides a real-life study of nature versus nurture.

Painting the Reality of My Soul

A Lifelong Journey of Verse

by

Cindy Lee Scott

with Alex Bennet

MQIPress (2020)

Frost, West Virginia

ISBN – 978-1-949829-34-1

MQIPress
Frost, West Virginia
303 Mountain Quest Lane, Marlinton, WV 24954
United States of America
Telephone: 304-799-7267
eMail: alex@mountainquestinstitute.com
www.mountainquestinstitute.com
www.mountainquestinn.com
www.MQIPress.com
www.Myst-Art.com

ISBN 978-1-949829-34-1
Cover photo by Cindy Lee Scott

Preface

Ah! What times we have lived through to bring us to today … the difficult-to-believe reality of a consciousness shift. Did we think it would come without our individual and collective contributions? Without expanding our understanding of duality? Without the fear, anger, and frustration—peppered with dots of boredom—enabling our emotional guidance system to fully appreciate joy, compassion, and love?

The learning! An amazing ability to turn and twist our thoughts and bodies to respond to emerging events and, eventually, to engage our thoughts and feelings to move into our dreams. And all of this is captured and expressed in the poetic streaming of Cindy Lee Scott, poetry and prose entangled with her deep experiences of life.

This is the developmental journey we are all on, what we call the Intelligent Social Change Journey, a journey of body, mind and heart, moving from the heaviness of cause-and-effect linear extrapolations, to the fluidity of co-evolving with our environment, to the lightness of breathing our thought and feelings into reality. This is very much a *social* journey, for change does not occur in isolation. The deeper our understanding in relationship to others, the easier it is to move into the future.

We explore these ideas at the Mountain Quest Institute, a research and retreat center situated in the Allegheny Mountains of West Virginia dedicated to the Quest for Knowledge, the Quest for Consciousness, and the Quest for Meaning. The Institute is scientific, humanistic, and spiritual, and finds no contradiction in this combination. Indeed, it is the holistic individual who has discovered the connections and relationships among these who is able to successfully navigate the changing landscape of humanity.

Cindy, who I have met only once in this physical life, has become the Poet Laureate of Mountain Quest Institute. Each of the 22 books titled *Possibilities that are YOU!* includes poetic prose from Cindy. These small Conscious Look Books are conversational in nature, taking full advantage of the reader's lived experience to share what can sometimes be difficult concepts. With the exploration of self facilitated through these ideas—supported by Cindy's verse—we are able to fully explore who we are and who we can become. With this exploration comes a glimmer of hope as we begin to reclaim the power of each and every mind developed by the lived human experience!

It is with appreciation and admiration that I join with Cindy to offer this collection of prose honoring her life and learning.

Dr. Alex Bennet
Mountain Quest Institute

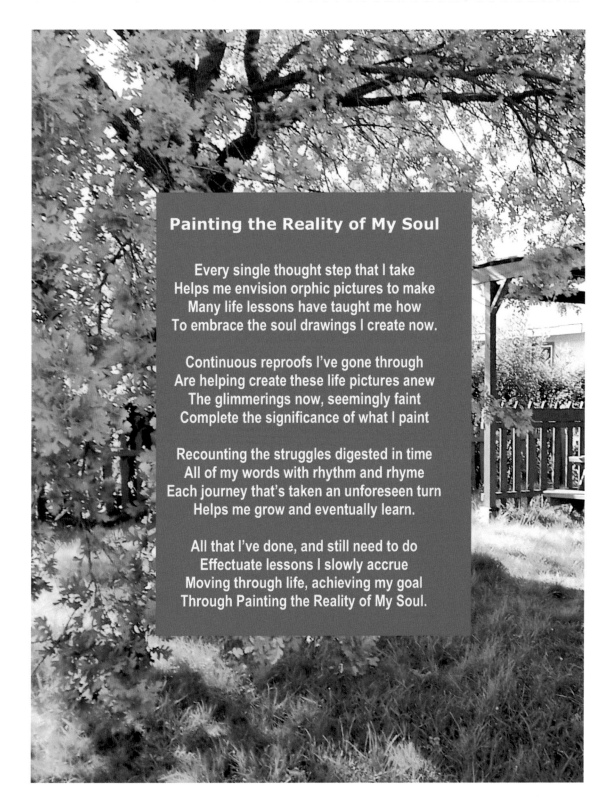

Painting the Reality of My Soul

Every single thought step that I take
Helps me envision orphic pictures to make
Many life lessons have taught me how
To embrace the soul drawings I create now.

Continuous reproofs I've gone through
Are helping create these life pictures anew
The glimmerings now, seemingly faint
Complete the significance of what I paint

Recounting the struggles digested in time
All of my words with rhythm and rhyme
Each journey that's taken an unforeseen turn
Helps me grow and eventually learn.

All that I've done, and still need to do
Effectuate lessons I slowly accrue
Moving through life, achieving my goal
Through Painting the Reality of My Soul.

Contents

Preface by Alex Bennet

How does one become a poet?

Looking back, what an incredible life I've had! It is most definitely overwhelming when reflecting on all the magnificent, as well as difficult, times I've been through. Yet, here I am still embracing life, fighting my battles, and growing in this never and ever-ending story of me. Dramas and comedies, sadness and elations, melancholy and exuberance, failures and victories, all forming the person I've become. While some of these ventures were difficult to embrace and exposed frailties, others fulfilled life-long dreams, allowing me to taste the fruits of my spirit.

It is the Yin and Yang, the good and bad, heaven and hell, the dark and the light, whatever your perception of the dynamic opposites in life are, all there to teach us. It is the understanding of both sides of life that truly helps us open our minds and grow.

I am so thankful for the friends and family along the way that were so patient with me … and I cannot help but remember what a very close friend once told me, that I appeared to be a "fluffy bunny in a hurricane" and oh what storms would occasionally come my way! And somewhere along that way, I moved into a continuous search for beauty through verse and prose.

Beauty births from unbridled violence
Coming from the dark void of silence
The world sparks matter coming alive
All things work together to survive.

In the planet's violent delirium
Everything sought equilibrium
Balancing the young earth, moon and sun
The road to life on earth had begun.

What is beauty? That's not an easy question to answer, because beauty means different things to different people. It is definitely based on the personal experiences of the individual. From the viewpoint of our senses, beauty is something good, pleasing, attractive and satisfying, a combination of qualities, impressive to touch, feel, look at, taste, smell, listen to and think about. It is that special state where something seems, well, *perfect*, at least from a personal point of view! If it's a sunset we are watching, there's just the right variety and amount of color. If it's the music we are listening to, the melody, tonal patterns and rhythm make my heart sing, or my head soar. If it's that special someone walking through my life …. Just use your imagination for that description!

One thing is consistent. The experience of beauty has the quality of transcendence. It is a "now" experience, and if you are fully engaged in the "now" of beauty, then there's little room for any of the negative energies from the past and present that periodically, and sometimes regularly, hang onto us. Think about this for a minute … if each of us pursued the goal of creating beauty, what an amazing world we would live in!

Oh, beautiful soul, love transcending
Feel freedom's truth ascending
Thoughts, feelings, actions take hold
Beaming beauty from within, behold.

Beauty is a multiplier, and art—a picture, a poem, a story—can touch so many people's hearts. This is the gift I have left to give. May this gift become yours.

Cindy Lee Scott, 2021

I. Birthing the Poet

EARTH AND SKY *(Age 10)*

I lay upon the sweet-smelling green grass, looking up
At the fluffy white clouds in a spring blue sky;
My arms open beside me holding onto the earth
As I watch the dotted clouds go speeding by.

Sunshine bathes the skin of my being with soothing warmth
And the cool air blows above and around me;
Directly below, my body joins with Mother Earth.
This changes the perception of what I see.

With eyes closed, the spinning motion intensifies
Am I sailing on an orbiting earth trip?
I feel stirring movement below, and figure out
I'm just a traveler on this planet ship.

Feelings soar with puffy clouds and I'm one with the sky
With the immense revolving earth below me;
Knowing that I've traveled while laying here on my back,
Yet not moving one muscle, how can this be?

Waking from my imagined journey, my body stiff,
It left me thinking how it would feel to fly
How did I sense the ground spinning round on its axis?
I guess I am just left just wondering why.

CINDY: All these feelings, and deep thoughts with no one to talk to … constantly reaching for understanding the foreign world around me. I needed to find a way to let those emotions out.

THE POET

My deepest thoughts I need to confide
All these whirling swirling feelings inside
Must find a way to facilitate
Reflections needed to communicate
Brought in focus through meditation
Idea's spurred by way of inspiration.

Feeling an urge to poeticize
Imagination tends to fantasize
Fastening the words so cleverly
Clearly lending the soul to reverie
Creating love's actuality
Word pictures of my soul's reality.

CINDY: Singing proved my earliest outlet, so much of my verse emerged with melody. I remember singing into a large empty coffee can, just trying to express myself, and, of course, always alone as not to be embarrassed. While the sound was muted, there was a delightful vibration within the can, and within me. Before long, I learned to play instruments, engaging first the harmonica, then the keyboard and guitar … grabbing hold of whatever I could make music with. Nothing ever seemed to be enough, but still I pushed forward, wanting to play music with anyone that would interact with me.

In my twenty's, I began to write down words in the form of poetry, as well as writing my songs. At first it was a struggle, and it seemed that as the lyrics and poems emerged, everything I wrote only left me with more questions and wonderings. However, the pain began to find escape.

I'm really glad I didn't throw those early writings away. They are my gage of life; they show me how much I've grown with all of my experiences and, of course, aging over the years.

Silent Soul Tears

Crying out for Momma, feeling lost and afraid
Memories of her face becoming a blurred fade
Help me find my Mommy, tell me where did she go?
When will she come back for me? This I do not know.

In sleep the small child cries out in soul wrenching pain
Innocence of heart blotched with a permanent stain
An overwhelming ache to feel her mother's arm
Who will hold and love her and keep this child from harm?

Loneliness and night fears become the child's new friend
Darkness brings nightmares that never seem to end
Many tearful months—times are quickly passing by
The emptiness inside has no more tears to cry.

The child-like smiling face hides pain pushed down deep
No longer calling out in endless weeping sleep
Yet loneliness and fear lay entombed inside for years
Slowly welling up, becoming Silent Soul Tears.

SOUL EYES

Far beyond what the eye can see
Deep within the spiritual me
Listen past the things that I hear
Wait for outside chatter to clear

Beyond what the emotions feel
Work very hard to see what's real
Look beyond this life drama show
Maybe I'll see what I need to know

My first experience with death was not of my own making. I remember not feeling well, being so tired and having my urine turn orange. I was aware something was wrong and while I was at work, I asked for a urinalysis. The Doctor or Pathologist I worked with looked concerned and asked me how I felt. He told me to go on home and someone would give me a call with the results. I had no idea what was to come.

I received a phone call at home and was told to go straight into the hospital where I was admitted and put into isolation. I was overwhelmed by the gowns, mask, head turbans and the booties the hospital personnel were all wearing. There were two doors into my hospital room with a small room between them. It was in that small room where the doctors, nurses and technicians would gown up. The second door made a loud suction noise when opened. The whole experience was extremely unnerving and I felt alone and frightened.

As soon as the blood work all came back it was found that my jaundice was not the contagious kind. Since my Hepatitis was not airborne, I would no longer be in isolation. I was scheduled for an X-ray with dye to check for possible gallstones, which could also cause jaundice. Then the unimaginable happened that would forever change me and my outlook on life!

A gurney arrived to take me to X-ray. It was nice to get out of that room even if it was only a trip through the hospital hallways. When I arrived, I was put on that hard X-ray table, grateful they allowed me to have a pillow. Another bag of fluid was hung to my existing IV and I was told it was dye to help the doctor see if I had any gallstones. Okay, at least I wasn't going to be stuck again. I noticed that one of the X-ray personnel was an actual Doctor and I asked him why he was there. He calmly said, anytime we insert a dye, we like to have a Doctor present. (A presentiment of what was to come.) Then, I heard the Doctor say, "We can begin now." I just lay there, trying to relax, watching a tech turn the switch allowing the fluid from the dye into my IV drip.

A strange feeling came over me, with the sensation becoming increasingly more intense! I was getting very concerned, but the only words I managed to get out of my mouth were: "Something's Wrong!" I felt a tingling in my feet and fingers and an electric feeling moving up my extremities. It was like the feeling you get after sleeping on your arm as it wakes up … a dead-like numbing followed by a harsh electric tingling.

I became overwhelmed with fear, the kind of fear that consumes the whole body, like stepping in front of a fast-moving bus. Frozen in that fear, I was paralyzed! The voices in the room were talking faster and faster; it was like a carnival and I was on the carousel! My last memory was of glass breaking and my arm being hit so hard, my whole body moved. Then, all the fear was gone.

I experienced a peace never had before, and there are no words to describe it. No pain. No cold. No hot. Pure tranquility. Everything quiet and dark; a darkness with no light. I sensed I was turning, using only thought, looking for a light from somewhere! Then I saw it; a pinpoint of light very far away. I needed that light; I sensed a great urgency to reach it. As I moved towards the light, it grew larger and larger. My need to get there increased the closer I came to it; and I was moving faster and faster! I was so close now; the light seemed to be within reach. My whole being marveled at this glorious, wondrous light, a bright white luminous energy like nothing I'd ever experienced! Words can't begin to describe it. THEN, IN AN INSTANT, I'm pulled back into my body.

DEATH UNEXPECTED

Oh, death's sting at such a tender age
Unexpected turn on this life stage
Passing through intensive walls of fear,
Loss of sight and can no longer hear.

Turning in the void, searching for light
Finding a pin point, shining so bright.
Drawn towards the illumined spot
Feeling no pain neither cold nor hot.

Just when reaching my destination
Pulled back to my life's restoration.
Parting absolute tranquility,
Awakening to fragility.

Returning from my recent demise,
Having witnessed death thru my soul eyes
A change in me I can clearly see
Life's finite end no longer scares me.

(continued from previous page)

I opened my eyes and was back on the X-ray table, surrounded by the doctor, nurses and technicians … and they were all staring at me. My body was a mass of pain. Every part of me hurt. When I was able to speak, I looked at the doctor and asked: "Is that what it feels like to die?" He looked back at me and said with a slight forced smile, "You tell me."

It was a long time before I was taken back to my hospital room, and the whole time I lay there thinking about what had just happened. I felt different now. My childhood fear of dying was gone … I understood that living in this world was just a matter of feeling various degrees of pain. The lowest degree may be torture and a high degree could be sensual. A middle degree might even be irritation. But all is pain compared to the afterlife; how else can we learn? *Without pain, we would not exist, so it needs to be embraced at all levels.*

EVERYTHING IS PAIN

No hot and no cold
Only pure serenity
Twisting and turning
A seamless infinity

In endless black void
Seeing beyond earthly sight
A bodiless me
Being drawn into the light.

Pulled back from death's door
The first breath drawn into me
Slowly functions return
Each pain, a different degree.

A most travailing
Awaking realization
Everything is pain
A Conceptualization.

KINGDOM OF THE BELLS

A people like I had never seen before
Folks sleeping all over and some on the floor
People were mostly friendly, and seemed so kind
That's just what I saw from my naïve young mind!

All extremely busy, with a happy face
This certainly appeared an exciting place
Dressed oddly different but not lost or forlorn
Are these the Hippies about which I've been warned?

All caring for this large Victorian home
In this four-floored commune, you're never alone
Some cleaned, some panhandled or traded their wares
Talking and laughing, they exhibited no cares.

Wearing macramé adorned with beads and shells
Braided cords hanging from the waistband with bells
As Hippies moved, I heard multi-pitched ringing
While others played instruments, with some singing.

From Florida to DC seemed a long way
To this magical place I wanted to stay
These so-called "evil" Hippies had much to give
The Kingdom of Bells is a fun place to live!

CUSTOMS

We hitched to Canada one summer
Crossed the border to visit a friend.
Didn't realize that we would be searched,
An ordeal I'd not go through again.

My baby's dirty cloth diapers were foul,
No place to rinse them while on the go;
Soiled ones placed in a large garbage bag,
That it would be searched we didn't know.

Searched us first, then saw the garbage bag
Border agents asked, "What's in that bag?"
Through the glass we watched as they checked
Each dirty diaper … and saw them gag.

The agent gave the bag back to me
And yuck! No longer did I want them.
He watched while I threw that bag away
And asked me why I did that to him.

I wish today to apologize
For what surely I put that man through.
If only I'd thought before feeling,
Because it really made me sick, too!

ALEX: From "Kingdom of the Bells" and "Customs" you can tell that Cindy lived the life of a flower child in the late 60's to early 70's, and with that all the wide-ranging experiences that come with a free spirit rebelling against structure and hunting for purpose. While I did not discover Cindy—or, rather, she did not discover me—until many years later, as a point of irony, while Cindy was tripping on LSD and dancing on the mall putting flowers in the ends of guns, I was working for the Federal government in the new Bureau of Drug Abuse Control setting up the library on Timothy Leary and cohorts. So many years later, it is hard to imagine how very close we must have come. I regularly walked across the mall, visiting museums at lunchtime, and climbing the stairs of the Washington Monument for exercise, and I wonder: On a sunny afternoon, did we ever unknowingly pass each other?

FLOWERS IN BARRELS

One on the corner of each block
All young men dressed in army green;
Martial soldiers standing erect,
Looking all the same when they're seen.

Holding that gun up by your side
Like statues standing in the sun;
Eyes not allowed to notice mine,
I put a flower in each gun.

Looking into each young man's eyes
A blank face with emotion's lack,
But still, I give a friendly smile
Unseen, one gives me a smile back!

GRAVEYARD PLAY

Moon just bright enough to run around in the dark
Amongst the well-kept trees and foliage in this park
The cool freshly cut grass under foot left no doubt
Perfect summer evening for frolicking about.

Running and playing like small children felt so
grand
In our own made-up world that's a fantasy land
Until hearing a startled voice calling for help
Something between a muffled guffaw and a yelp!

Moving towards the troubled trembling voice, still
laughing
Finding him in a newly dug hole was baffling
Pulling him out of the hole was an easy save
Until realizing, it was a freshly dug grave.

Our phantasm was happening in a graveyard
Navigating the graves on the way out was hard
Contemplating quietly on the way home, we found
Our demeanor had become soberingly sound

Tripping in a graveyard

FLOWER CHILD

The essence of the Flower Child
Lacking real love, she goes wild
Seeking all that's missing inside
My blinded eyes open wide
Bathing in the warmth of the sun
Soul searching, child on the run
Waiting for Aquarian days
Offers love in many ways ...

The Hippiness of youth lingers as we age!

Drawing by Cindy Taylor

SECRET PACT

Afraid, wounded hold tightly to each other
They can be strangers, siblings, or a mother.
Purpose is given by holding on so tight,
Trying to hide from the inward pain and fright.

Predators create fear to control the weak
It is safety and refuge that victim's seek.
Lost lambs live in fear with deep-seeded loathing,
Under the power of wolves in sheep clothing.

An unknown enemy lurks on the outside;
Only one another in whom to confide.
An unspoken bond is a matter of fact;
The world held together by a Secret Pact.

TIES THAT BIND

Breaking free, creating incitement,
Mixed feelings of fear and excitement.
Keeping pain inside through carousing;
Found my new world in flux arousing.

When my reality was shaken,
Gathering items to be taken,
I would leave all that I knew behind,
Tearing and breaking those Ties That Bind.

Endless Roads

Oh, endless roads presumed different placing;
Paths seem to be always and ever changing.
Many cities, but the routes all look the same;
Never-ending roads, each with a different name.

Passing scenes lulling one to a peaceful trance;
Each landscape seems to have its own special dance.
Potholes in the broken roads keep one awake;
We bounce around with a tumble and a shake.

The feeling of freedom cannot be denied;
Offering excitement that we cannot hide.
Exploring each artery to discover
An amazing closeness to one another.

ALEX: There were unintended consequences associated with this lifestyle, which brought with them intense moments of learning, and added an urgency to the thoughts and emotions bursting forth from the poet becoming. While I did not live them, through her verse these shared moments have provided insights into Cindy's life such that I have been better able to understand the roles of nature and nurture. And this synergistic connection with the poetry of Cindy's life has enabled me to learn so much more about myself.

FACE OF HATRED

Oh, hooded figures 'round the fire
I cannot believe that's what I see;
Something inside does not feel right,
Face of hatred in front of me!

Many robes of white bearing tall
Covered faces cannot be seen;
Can't perceive what's in front of me
From the naïve view of sixteen.

Opening sight to perception,
Seeing this world from youthful eyes.
Don't understand how this can be?
Innocence lost, my spirit cries.

OVERDOSE

Fragile life hanging by a thread
Life forces holding on to you;
Reposing in death's restful hold
There is much left for you to do.

Ready to leave this unkind world
With all its battles to be won;
Pulled back from the brink of death's door
For my time here is not yet done!

CINDY: The demonstration was over and I walked the busy streets asking for spare change from strangers to feed my baby. The hungrier I got, the more I fed little "Root Beer". He was starting to get chubby and I was getting thinner. Not eating much was starting to impact my body. I remember thinking that all I wanted was for my baby to be alright, but my mind wasn't so clear anymore ….

In the afternoon, I would contact the Switchboard. On this particular evening, I was given the name and phone number of two young men that lived in a Victorian basement flat below a business. These two young men allowed me to stay in their living room area with my son for a few days. In the evenings after the business was closed, I would set up my baby's playpen. This is where little Root slept and I would lay on the floor beside the playpen using my coat as a pillow and drift off to sleep. I had lost my job and left my home; now, look where I was at. I was so tired nowadays, and if not for the kindness of strangers where would I be? It seemed as if my whole life was a series of one kind of abandonment after another! I know now that I really did not know any other way to live. This is what I knew and what I was used to. So much pain; just push it down and keep on going! That was my only plan. What else could I do? What else did I know?

(Continued on next page)

On about the third day while I was panhandling, I was approached by a pleasant man who had something he thought I would enjoy: he gave me a (four-way hit) of mescaline. I was not familiar with this drug but knew that I was living in a world full of new Hippie "enlightenments" and wanted desperately to be a part of the "Age of Aquarius." What I did not know was how powerful a drug mescaline is. I also did not understand that a four-way hit was meant to be divided among four people. I took the whole capsule, lay down beside the play pen Root was already asleep in, and waited for the pill to set my mind free. What I did not realize is that I had overdosed!

Root continued sleeping soundly beside me in his play pen. The room was dark, and the moonlight was shining through the windows. A gentle evening breeze was blowing through the open windows. I fell asleep watching the white translucent curtains rolling in the breeze, or so I thought.

All around me was darkness, complete darkness. Then I was above my body looking at myself lying on my back with my eyes closed. I was slowly fading away and surrendering to much-needed sleep. I had been so tired, and this felt so good. It was getting harder to breathe; it would be much easier to just let go. Somewhere in my head I began to understand that my spirit was slipping away from my body! This was not my first brush with death. I felt no pain and I was not afraid, I've been here before. It's okay, I told myself. Life is just too hard! *I'm tired of fighting all the battles going on inside and outside. I just want to be released from my prisons ...* Now breathing was becoming too difficult, so I let go and waited, waiting for the light to draw me in.

It was in this moment of waiting that an audible voice filled the space around me, seeming to come from all directions. A powerful but kind "all encompassing" voice spoke to me saying: *Take a breath ... Your Time Here Is Not Done!* Somehow, that voice gave me the strength to fill my lungs with air. As my lungs expanded, it was as if I were singing! Then, as the air left my lungs, I began to fade again. *I'm so tired and I just want to rest.* Again, the voice repeated, *Breathe ... Your Time Here Is Not Done. You have more to do.*

Again, I filled my lungs with air, focused on the voice that kept me breathing. This went on for I'm not sure how long. As the voice spoke to me, I could hear the wind blowing and loud noises, as if things were breaking. Then I slept a deep, non-dreaming sleep.

When I awoke, it was morning and the sun was shining. The front and back doors of the flat were wide open. Things were moved and the room in disarray. One of the screens on the front windows was ripped open! Beside me was baby Root, still asleep. He had slept through the whole night. What happened? As I looked around it seemed as if all Hell had broken loose! And this is where my life changed.

It was not until later in my life that I understood the significance of what had happened to me. I couldn't understand then the things in my life that needed to be done, that I had many roads ahead of me to travel and four more special "little spirits" to come into my life. I couldn't even have imagined what was ahead of me and how I would finally embrace life (the pain and the joy), instead of running from it. I had no idea just how many of my dreams would come true. Now I understand that *my time here, truly, was not done!*

And the lessons continued.

SETTLED

In this intensely turbulent world
We must ever practice to stay calm
Being caught up in the chatter is easy
When listening to the hoopla song.

Keep your eye on the bigger picture
As for the drama, just say "I won't"
There're problems needing your attention
Needless to say, there are some that don't.

Turbulent souls do not have answers
And those vexed unsettled spirits wane;
So, embrace repose in your endeavors
From the humongous to the mundane.

RAIN

Oh, the rain, like nature's tears,
Are just like tears of our own.
The rain comes to help us grow;
Leads us to paths yet unknown.

As the rain washes the earth,
So do our tears wash the soul.
Our time on earth will soon pass,
And be like in days of ole.

For each teardrop that does fall
Converges in pools of time.
It deepens our growth in love
And ages us like good wine.

Those who could not bear the tears,
With their lessons to bestow,
The shallow life they will lead
Won't really help them to grow.

So, I say, my weary friend,
Do take those lessons with strife,
And look to your soul for tears.
They'll teach about love and life.

Oh, the rain, like nature's tears,
Are just like tears of our own.
The rain comes to help us grow
And leads us to paths unknown.

CINDY: Raising a family was the most satisfying of all the ventures in life I've taken on. During this time, I did the most growing emotionally as well as mentally. I filled that lonely, empty space inside of me with children that loved me giving back the amazing amount of love I had for them. That's when I finally grew up and matured.

BOOGIE ON DOWN

Boogie on Down, Come on boogie on;
Boogie around, Come on boogie on;
Boogie on Down, Come on boogie on;
Boogie around, Come on boogie on.

Hey little girl dancing all over;
She shakes it one way, then the other.
Watch my little girl spin round and round;
I know she's watching it all come down.

I know you were sent from God above;
See the big smile that she gives to me.
It fills my heart with such a great love;
You'll break many a heart, wait and see.

Boogie on Down

MOTHER'S DAY

When tired, challenged
And sometimes just struggling,
Managed each child's needs
With some creative juggling.

Through both the blunders
And nurturing elations,
My five children were
My greatest motivations.

From the bottom of my heart
I'd just like to say:
I celebrate my children

Every Mother's Day.

ROCK-A-COUCH

Three small children together sitting close to me.
All fit that old, worn blanket-covered-over-seat.
One on each side of me, the smallest in my lap,
Pushing that wood-framed rocker with both of my feet.

One under each of my arms, one next to my heart;
What a wonderful feeling me holding all three.
A lingering nostalgic cherished memory
Holding all my babies forever close to me.

FRED THE CAKE

Would you like to meet my friend, Fred the Cake?
He will greet you with a big smile.
Whether you're tired, sleepy or wide-awake,
Fred will visit you for a while.

Now, if you thought you'd like to be his friend,
Too late, because someone ate Fred.
A knife brought him to such a dreadful end.
It's so sad that our Fred is dead!

MOCKINGBIRD SONG

Mockingbirds are always listening,
Watching all that we do.
Trying to repeat what they see
And what they hear from you.

If Mockingbirds hear hurtful words
With a stern, stinging shout,
The pain inside begins to build
And then anger comes out.

The Mockingbirds only repeat
Expressions that were sown.
Unkind words can leave them afraid,
And feeling all alone.

The little birds speak up needing
Just to be understood
While love gets lost in the world of
Just trying to be good!

SIMPLER TIMES

Darkness fades the unending blue void
In the vastness of an unknown deep
A faint cool breeze drifts through the window
Rhythmic crickets lull younglings to sleep.

The tunes of morning song birds break forth
Announcing the emerging new day
Barefoot children run through the cool grass
Engaged in jubilant summertime play.

Larking hide and seek, making up games
Chasing rainbows little ones' rollick
Carefree days pass ever so endless
Life moves on as innocents frolic.

CINDY: After my children were gone, I faced a challenging and sobering period of my life. I began to create more than I had ever before, learning some new skills on the synthesizer. Yes, I took keyboard lessons in my fifties, and did quite well now that my mind had become so much clearer. This was a strongly creative and very fruitful part of my life, and I enjoyed being a part of the church praise team playing the synthesizer, adding heartful expression to the overall sound of the music. This was a dream come true, something I had always wanted to do. And it had finally happened, but, then, life always moves on; nothing ever stays the same. As we move from an external focus to an internal focus, so, too, do our lifelines shift.

GROUNDED

You are grounded when
You're born in this carnal world
And cradled against a loving breast.

You are grounded when
A caregiver who loves you,
Reaches to pick you up when you fall.

You are grounded when
Choosing to have a family,
They become the center of your world.

You are grounded as
Time drains the fervor of youth
Growing in wisdom till that last breath.

Finally, you're grounded
When a reveal to the soul
Shows the path that's waiting after death.

CINDY: As I moved into my sixties, Parkinson's began to take its toll on me. It sapped my strength, and I lost the ability to play up on a stage. Even working in my garden became near impossible. For a couple of years, my youngest daughter, who was a worship leader, and my son-in-law would set up my equipment at church so I could continue to play with the praise team. What a beautiful thing it was watching my daughter and her husband lead worship. It was a wonderful experience, and the mere thought today brings a smile within!

So, I celebrated life.

Parkinson's

As stiffness in my body grows, what's left of my strength wains
I make it to the bedroom chair, still leaning on those canes
Collapsing down into that chair and taking a deep breath
I wonder if it ends that way, this final trek towards death?

Remembering, I realize, I'm still here for a reason
Immersion in that moment was only for a season
This tiresome pattern fills up the first hour of my day
And if perhaps you would not mind, there's more I'd like to say

From all of our experience, there's always more to learn
Sometimes it's not so easy, it takes patience to discern.
A smile, a funny thought, laughing through disabilities,
Little things I do myself show my capabilities

Instead of self-reflecting on what Parkinson's has taken,
I celebrate each precious day as slowly I awaken.

CINDY: In that celebration, my son jumped in to build me a Garden Sanctuary, which became a special place of joy for everyday renewal. Enter into this sanctuary with me through pictures and verse ... you are most welcome!

GARDEN SANCTUARY

My children were growing up and leaving one by one
On a journey to begin their own lives
In the backyard where many memories had been made
I see only shadows of family
A damaged pool with a broken-down deck and an old porch
Where we all gathered to sit down and talk.

Now where do I go with these remnants of the day's past
And loneliness that permeates the soul
With nature my solace, I stand next to the sole tree
We planted in the yard so long ago
It was as if nature spoke; I knew we needed more
Then just one tree standing strong in this yard.

I started designing a Garden Sanctuary
Where my spirit could finally find peace
With nature being one of my greatest joys in life
It would offer a place for me to rest
The Garden Sanctuary would bring quiet solace
To the restless and yearning soul within.

My son labored hard with the sweat running down his face
As he dredged the earth to create a pond
The edges of the pond had a boarder of shad stones
Placed to look as natural as they could
Water lilies and other plants flourished in the pond
With a flowing waterfall at one end.

The baby Koi fish were placed in the completed pond
They were all so beautiful and peaceful
Under the water we gave them a small stoneware house
To have a safe place to keep the fish warm
We put an old black metal rocker beside the pond,
And I spent hours just watching fish grow.

Down came the old metal pool with the broken liner
Which was cut into amenable pieces
Some boards were fashioned to resemble slats on a fence
And attached to the wooden half-round deck
Then the deck and the fence were painted the same color,
And the stairs were rebuilt with plants on top.

Brick by brick, we laid paths meandering through the yard
Visions bursting forth from a simple wish
A sycamore tree was planted where the pool had been
With a path of stone laid around the tree
A swing was placed in one corner of the circle path
With pillows for taking a peaceful nap.

The back porch was made to look like an old wood cabin
And lots of chimes were hung around the top
With sounds, smells and touch and even the tasting of herbs
Sensing nature from all parts of the yard
For many years I looked forward to meditating
In my blessed Garden Sanctuary.

CINDY: Eventually, as is so with aging, it was all too much. I had to sell my house and move into an apartment. This was a new experience ... that year was the only time in my life that I had ever lived totally alone. While my children were a great comfort, they had active lives of their own. Fortunately, my next-to-the-youngest daughter and her baby lived in the same apartment complex. She and my grandchild would come over after work, and while I played with the baby, she would prepare dinner for us all. My other grown children would visit every week or so. What a blessing to have such wonderful children.

Having so much time to myself, I began going through my music and old writings, and even started writing a guitar chord book. That was an enormous job and took a lot of my time. I kept thinking that I'd be able to play again, but it did not work out that way, which I eventually had to come to grips with.

I started getting in touch with my siblings and even talked to my stepfather. Now that my mother had passed, my stepfather gave me a bit of information about my two brothers that had been adopted when I was around three years old. This stired my interest once again to begin searching for my two brothers, as well as the two sisters, that had been adopted out. Anyway, that's another story for another time.

After about a year in that apartment complex, my daughter and I decided to look for a house to rent together, someplace where Baby Sebastian, now four, could grow up and have a little room to run and play. This was perfect for all three of us. I was having a difficult time getting around caring totally for myself, and as Sebastian got older, I could keep an eye out for him when his Mom had to work and he had no school. Did I mention how much fun it is being a Grandmother!

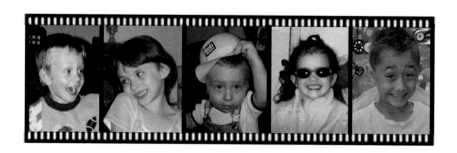

A CHILD'S WISH

A child saw a dandelion seeding in the green grass,
Making a wish, he blew those seeds up into the wind.
I ask about the wishes he had made as we pass,
Strolling on this spring day, just trying to be a friend.

His very first wish was that his Daddy would stop smoking
The next wish was that Dad's girlfriend didn't have to die.
All that he was saying seemed truly thought provoking
It deeply saddened me, and brought a tear to my eye.

I asked that if he had a third wish, what would it be?
He wished Grandma was not old, and once again could walk.
While momentarily awestruck, his deep wisdom I could see
I reassured him I was glad that we'd had this talk.

The little child spoke
    what he felt from his gentle heart,
An innocence within
    so pure, so benevolent.
If only men could hear
    what this young child could impart,
We'd truly understand
    what in life is relevant!

Drawing by Benjamin Mankin

WHY DID YOU WAKE ME UP?

The holidays are over and the evening has come
Mom has got to work tomorrow, and she is feeling numb.
Her son climbs into bed with her; there's no school tomorrow
"Be quiet" she whispers, thinking about work with sorrow.

As sleep finally comes over the Mom, needing her rest,
The son is still excited, feeling Christmas was the best.
More than once Mom has to call out, "Please let me sleep!"
The boy's eyes fill with tears, and then they flow down his cheek.

The boy asks his Mom, "Why do you yell so loudly at me?"
Mom responds, "I have to work and need my sleep. Can't you see?"
The little boy calms down, not wanting to interrupt,
"But Mommy, I don't yell like that when *you* come wake *me* up."

CINDY: As I was cleaning out an old memory trunk, I found a bunch of old writings from my twenties, as well as a hand-printed version of the story of my life as I remembered it. As I entered those old poems and songs into the computer, it began stirring up deep feelings, and I needed to write again. While correcting those old poems, I found a strong desire to write down what I was now feeling and what I had learned over the years. So, it began, and I liken it to a volcano blowing after being held back for so long. That creative part in me was not over! Life had just taken another turn, and I had gone full circle! I was writing and writing, and found that in those quiet times when alone, some of my most inspirational moments happened.

Instead of trying to shut life out from all I thought I had lost, I began to tune in, discovering my time here was not yet done. I still had more to give and receive. AND THAT IS HOW THIS BOOK CAME TO BE! Now, in my seventies and looking back, it seems that all I ever needed to do was seek and find what was waiting for me just around the bend. **The birthing of a poet appears to be a lifelong journey of becoming** … and so let's become together.

PEARLS OF WISDOM

Pearls of Wisdom are shown to us throughout
Our life-long traveling course.
Share them with others so that in the end
You'll not have burdened remorse.

The life lessons learned, as we age, are like
Beautiful pearls made from sand,
Made with a lifetime of bumps and bruises
Incited by our own hand.

When we keep all our lessons to ourselves
Then life's children cannot learn.
This compels mistakes to repeat again
As those same problems return.

You might think that no one actually wants
To hear what you've got to say.
Maybe not now, but there may come a time
When they'll need to find their way.

Those insightful Pearls of Wisdom can help
Our progeny to evolve,
Giving hope in the coming Earth crisis
Our children will need to solve.

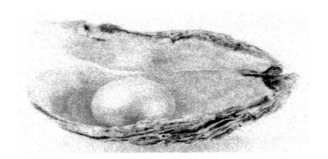

THESE HANDS

These Hands, they reached out for help when I was young
Gathering the love needed to grow.
They helped me understand the world I was in
And the things that I needed to know.

These small hands sensed what was good, and what was not
With a fundamental need called touch,
So, on I grew, and these hands became stronger
Steadily absorbing, gleaning much.

These strong hands began to play the piano
This made music "a big part of me,"
And that was only the beginning of how
Singing and dance set my spirit free.

And when these hands learned to strum the folk guitar
I sang to my heart's budding desire.
Getting older, these hands reached out, seeking love
As my glowing heart was set afire.

Gentle hands held my sweet children in my arms
And close to my breast as each was born.
When hurt, wiped away their tears, comforting them
Until night brought on the break of morn.

Sturdy hands sewed blankets and clothes for the kids
We often sat on the floor to play.
I taught my children everything that I knew
And would have had it no other way.

These stout hands dug gardens, growing food to eat
And herbs for making my soups and stew.
As the children grew up and left, I fashioned
A Sanctuary from all I knew.

For many years these hands continued working
'Till my legs they could no longer stand.
Countless hours were spent in Sanctuary
Creating with these weary old hands.

Getting older, disease tore at my body
I could no longer work in the yard.
Turning to music, these hands played once again
Until that also became too hard.

These tired hands started to sort lyrics and verse
From younger times, when I still could stand.
And now what's in my heart is all that is left
Free flowing through the pen in my hand.

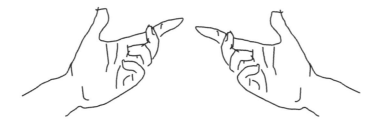

CINDY: *There is a River of Knowing.* The intuitive mind's eye sees far beyond images. The perceptive listener hears beyond the spoken word. The soul reflective empath feels the truth beyond emotion. The discerning clairvoyant looks beyond appearances. When combined, all of these senses embrace the *River of Knowing.*

EMERGENCE

Slowly emerging come the freshly sprouted seed plants
Fighting their way upward through newly fertilized Earth
Ever pushing up towards the beckoning spring warmth
With illumined morning sunlight nurturing their birth.

It's the wonderment of so many countless spawning's,
Bursting forth hope for all the coming generations,
That have surely flourished here so many times before
With all of their grand and glorious variations.

So do our Soul Seeds continuously sprout and grow,
Traveling on towards that expanding, beckoning light
That lay in us dormant and ready to germinate
As Earthly incarnate souls gain intuitive sight.

Experience expands our spiritual discernment
Forever perfecting a budding embodied peace,
Bringing with it optimistic hope and lasting faith
For the utopian future when the soul finds release.

II. Escaping our Prison

Innocence of Heart

Oh, for the innocence of the heart,
So vulnerable to manipulation,
Gullible to charismatic intellectuals,
That fill the lamb with jubilation.

The naive trust the knowledgeable schemer,
Sitting upon a visionary's imagined throne,
Giving enlightenment with the jaded word,
Asking the susceptible to give all they own.

Simple minded, unsuspicious of the teachings,
Impervious to how vulnerable they may be.
Unpretentious in receiving information,
Believing and accepting what they see.

Raven with the Dark Piercing Eyes

What's behind that look coming directly from you,
Oh, Raven with the Dark Piercing eyes.
It appears that you know some deep truth about me,
that slices through the deepest of lies.

Your accentuated stare and majestic stance
Appear to reach in and touch my soul,
I'm enthralled with your fiercely mesmerizing poise,
sitting on your pedestal so bold.

What truth do you bring to unfold in me today?
Are there more weeds in my heart to hew?
I ready an awakening within my soul
Without doubt I've more planting to do.

As I search and look inward for weeds to uproot
Listening to your penetrating cries,
I am grateful for this inspired visitation
Oh, Raven with the Dark Piercing Eyes.

Drawing by Lenore Joans

STINKING THINKING

Wondering why the ship is sinking
With that cynical Stinking Thinking?
A life filled with vain pessimism
Brings a lifetime of defeatism!
Sometimes all we need,
Is a change in attitude!

FOREVER VICTIM

A good portion of my misspent youth was consumed
Looking for someone to save me.
I had no cognition of what I was doing,
Quite simply, my eyes could not see.
I held on to my rescuer 'til they would tire
Underneath such encumbered strain
All that attention would become quite a burden
When bearing all my victim pain.

A Forever Victim often attracts others
That live in a similar way
A lifetime Forever Victim evolves to be
A predator, or easy prey.
Spiritual growth becomes stunted by the lessons
When a victim declines to learn.
Roads don't get easier, becoming more complexed,
With each and every twist and turn.

Staying a Forever Victim spirals downward
In a grim never-ending loop.
Encouraging other victims to follow you,
Forming a co-dependent group.
The circle repeats itself again and again
'til finally learning to forgive.
It's the forgiving and the being forgiven,
That teaches our heart how to live!

ALEX: I will jump in here to help provide some situational context beyond the words and feelings conveyed in verse. Now, you may wonder at the detail I am able to provide or, indeed, about my passionate interest in this work and its author. Perhaps you have guessed or read the introduction to Cindy's first published volume, *Rising Consciousness through Disruption and Corruption* (MQIPress, 2019). As I shared then, Cindy is a gift in my life, and through our almost daily conversations and Cindy's poetry, I have really, truly gotten to know this beautiful soul from the inside-out, and in the journey gained a deeper glance into who I am. But my appreciation of Cindy goes far beyond the unique and talented poet she has become. You see, when Cindy found me four years ago, she had been searching for a very long time. While I did not know she existed, she knew about me. I was adopted as an infant, and Cindy is my sister.

Cindy's life has been full. Living the life of a flower child, a young and naive Cindy moved geographically and emotionally in and out of life-challenging—and sometimes life threatening—situations. With her victimhood embroiled in fear and pain, she repeated patterns over and over again, seeking refuge in relationships and drugs, which opened the door to the next cycle of fear and pain. Then, finally, from the bottom of the rabbit hole, there was a glimmer of light, which appeared first as a distant potential but, in reality, was welling up inside of her, urging her to take responsibility for her life and emerge from the prisons of her mind.

PRISONS OF MY MIND

Meandering on my journey through life
Upon this unbridled anthropic plain
To so many evils vulnerable
Offering a life of consuming pain.

Playing the victim, befriending torment
Knowing this familiar spirit so well
Then one day awakening in a dark place
Drowning in my very own man-made hell.

Struggling in vain, stifled thoughts reach out
A passage through suffering I must find
Ensconced in battle I could not perceive
I'd become a prisoner of my own mind.

Playing the victim persona so well,
Living it over and over again
Bathed in sorrow, with anger lashing out,
Beckoning battles I could never win.

Relentless pleading for someone to help
Wallowing in pools of paralyzed fear.
Telling of anguishing, upending tales
Which my deafened ears could no longer hear.

Embracing and facing my deepest thoughts,
My inner eyes opened and I could see
The role of victim would dwindle away
By giving release to those who hurt me.

I must also forgive myself for pain
Which I've caused as I journey down the road
Judgment gives way to compassion and grace
That unburdened and lightened my load.

And with this release the answers grew clear:
To cultivate love and learn how to give
So now this worn body began to heal
And my burdened Soul was set free to live.

As I go on through this journey of life
With its numerous lessons left to find.
I sing! I soar! I've empowered release
And freedom from the prisons of my mind.

THE FALL

Tragedy happens to one and all.
It's not how many times you fall
When drinking from life's bitter cup
It's how many times you get back up!

Photo by Raiann Insogna

SLIPPING AWAY

Slipping in, slipping away
Drifting in a slumber state;
Being pulled into a lull
Just a malingering fate?

Unable to awaken
But not really quite asleep
Waking just for a moment
Then returning to the deep.

Many hours go drifting by
This drunken state still grips me
For time has no meaning here
In this soupy, dream-like sea.

Slipping in and slipping out
No longer know what to feel
Finding myself wondering
And pondering, what is real?

CINDY: "Slipping away" was written after an experience I had during a quiet meditation. I knew that I was in my recliner in the living room, but also felt as I was somewhere else that was new to me that I could not identify. After the experience was over, I quickly wrote it down so I wouldn't forget. Usually, when something of an unknown nature happens during meditation, it is my sub-conscious trying to contact my conscious. Occasionally I learn what it means right away, and other times it can take days, months or even years before clarity or a full understanding comes. What I'm trying to say is, it's always good to write dreams and experiences down, for life has an abundance of life lessons for us to learn. And no matter the age, we're still learning!

SPIRIT AND THE FLESH

Have you ever wondered why, after a weak moment
You felt, "Come on now, I should have known?"
Why did you carry on that way with this life lesson?
You know how many times you've been shown.
Yet, you go and repeat the mistakes over again,
Wondering, "Is this the curse of man?"
For weakness in the flesh is a strength in the spirit,
Which is a truth I now understand.

Now, whenever you feel an inner turmoil coming
And the world seems to be upside down,
That's when you start pleading for needed peace to return,
For the drama to not come around.
Give serious thought to the concept that, just maybe,
The battle's happening inside of you
For when the spirit and the flesh war with each other
It brings havoc to all that we do.

When the flesh is weak and you're meandering around
In all the places you should not go
You are pulled in with an irresistible fervor,
Feeling high first, and then feeling low.
By the weakened flesh you are tempted while being drawn
To what your spirit knows is not right.
Unbeknownst to you, the spirit and flesh are at war
In a perpetual everlasting fight!

DEPRESSION

Feeling so enormously heavy
Gloom in every direction I look
This draining weight is holding me down
A demon more than once I have shook.

There is a war going on inside
Manifesting paralyzing cries
A war between the flesh and spirit
Seen only with ethereal eyes.

Emotions

Emotions unpredictable
Often somewhat despicable
It's very difficult to see
How you have such a hold on me.

Never knowing when it will end
Swaying back and forth in the wind,
Riding the current ebb and flow
Capricious hormones, let me go!

CINDY: How easy it is to see now, the battle raging within between the physical, the mental, the emotional and the spiritual! The good news is that eventually some light of understanding crept in.

RIVER OF EMOTION

Riding the undulating River of Emotion
Flowing downward into a collective ocean
Rising above the energy fervor
Becoming a distant observer.
Seeking a reflective thought deliberation
Rising to a higher conscious liberation.

WORTH

Superannuated
Or just antiquated,
Worn out and obsolete.
Hanging back, out of beat.
Wisdom legitimized;
Worth is realized.

Learning from Mistakes

EARTH BOUND NETHER

The time is here for us
All to come together
Rising on upwards from
This earthly bound nether
Searching for needed truth
Thru our knowledge sharing
Collaborating world views
With co-creation pairing.

Openness and freedom
Of intuitive thought
Bring cooperation
Through the creation sought.
Streaming out to others
Cognition will soon come
In expanding spirals
Essential to wisdom!

ONE HOMINID TRIBE

Looking forward to an approaching future
A generation when all know for sure
That we all belong to the same human seed
And Earthly mortals are just one mixed breed

Maybe then, we will finally get along
Instead of advocating "right and wrong"
We'll celebrate, laying differences aside,
Realizing we are One Hominid Tribe!

TRUTH PREVAILS

With all of the commotion and confusion

Sanity and calmness wait behind the veil

Although angry and hateful voices ring loud

Ultimately, resounding truth will prevail!

STAIRWAYS

Another climb
Needing love's passion
Exposing all
Soliciting compassion

Showing your heart
Surrounding danger
Oh, so trusting
To a relative stranger.

Step by step invoking love
Climbing stairways to their end
Searching for a family
What I really need: a friend.

Streaming out to others
Cognition will soon come
In expanding spirals
Essential to wisdom!

ALEX: In this journey of becoming, there is a cyclical nature to life, which we can think about in terms of a spiral, ever learning and growing, yet similar situations emerging again and again until we discover the lesson and learn to make the best choices for ourselves and how we impact others.

LIFE CIRCLES

Sitting and staring at a warm fire,
Ridding the mind of invading thought,
Releasing unwarranted desire
And mental battles from within fought.

Letting go of vicious Life Circles
Of latent accusations and blame,
Peace comes offering a welcome gift
In this unrelenting circle game.

My mind relaxes to the rhythm
All consumed by the flickering light,
Bringing an inward calm to my soul
Illuminating my path so bright.

FOOD FOR THOUGHT

If just one person's perceived heaven
Is another man's torment,
And if one person's horror becomes
Another man's firmament,
Can there be only one rendering
Of a human's eternal home?

When a nation of various thoughts
Has beliefs globally known,
How narrow-minded is the thinking
That there's only one answer?
It's like giving a grand recital
And having just one dancer!

WAKING UP

Trying to grasp that which is not understood
Unending old sufferings
Opening eyes to observing the unseen
Spurring new awakenings.

Seeing the part played in the drama of life
Giving rise to awareness
Finding peace through insightful agape love
Knowing total forgiveness.

III. Living Life

LIFE PATHS

As I traveled through my life
I came upon four doors.
Was hard to choose between them
I wondered: Are there more?

Take the time to contemplate
The journeys that you choose.
Paths you take are not about
Whether you win or lose.

I'm older and I now know
All doors lead the same place.
The paths picked are the teachers,
The lessons in life's race.

ALEX: This idea of choice slips into Cindy's poetry again and again, as if she was trying to, at first, convince herself, and later confirming and strengthening her individuated power to choose, a self-empowering. Yet this serious focus emerges amidst the capturing of the playful, challenging, and reflective moments associated with a life well-lived.

HAPPY EVER AFTER EVENT

In stories with a happy-ever-after ending
Like those from our childhood past
Following the ending, looking beyond the story,
The happiness never lasts.
In "real" real life, the "happily ever after's" are
Fleeting emotions in time.
We eagerly accept these treasured moments in life,
I know that I do in mine.

What I'm actually trying to get across here is
"Life's not always what it seems".
I could even go as far as to say that sometimes
"We're living life in our dreams."
Even if we wake up, or even when we don't,
Maybe what I really meant,
It would be better if we said that we're having a
"Happy Ever After Event".

CHRISTMAS MEMORY TREE

Old Christmas tree ornaments of days gone by
With tinsel, lights and pretty ribbons that tie
Trinkets with jingles and silver bells that chime
Each memory seemingly frozen in time!

Years of hearts reaching out to one another
Dearest father, mother, sister and brother
Grandparents, daughters, sons, and all sorts of
blends
And let's not forget acquaintances and friends!

Sharing many stories while trimming the tree
Warmed within, glowing hearts are filled with glee
Hanging up all those vintage memories that last
Burned deep into the soul from Christmases past.

EVER CHANGING HEART

Emotional heart changing persistently
Must cautiously be guarded consistently
Hurtful words quickly scald a heart's tenderness
Damaging emotion's precious innocence.

Wisdom or hardness, what is the heart to do?
Changing seems the only real option for you
Hardheartedness makes room for anger and rage
While the ever-changing heart sets a new stage.

Through guidance and molding of the attitudes,
Seeking growth beyond emotion's platitudes,
It's never too early or too late to start
Nourishing growth of the ever-changing heart.

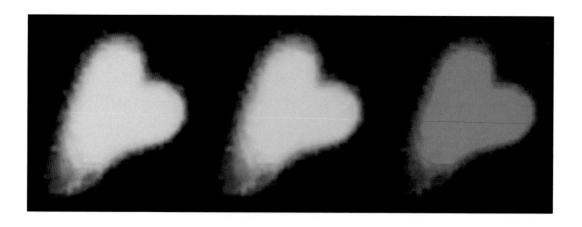

BALANCING THE HEART AND MIND

How does one balance the emotional heart
With the logical intellect mind?
Between passion and mind the harmony flow
Is not always easy to find.

For I physically hang out in a body
of brief temporal carnality
While I'm peering into the peculiar realm
of my spiritual reality.

Armed with the various learned lessons of self
With awareness of where I've come from;
Helps me discern the tribulations of life
And those I have yet to overcome.

Now I physically hang out in a body
of brief temporal carnality
While I'm peering into the peculiar realm
of my spiritual reality.

Somewhere along the way there's understanding
Of the path down which I am going;
Narrowing my focus so I can expedite
My conscious spiritual growing.

Still, I physically hang out in a body
of brief temporal carnality
While I'm peering into the peculiar realm
of my spiritual reality.

BABY KITTY

At six weeks of age Baby Kitty was attacked
By a very large dog, you see
With her small head in the dog's mouth the poor kitty
Was shaken very violently
After that attack, when she came to live with me,
She just was never quite the same
I washed her and removed several hundred fleas,
Then thought about giving her a name.

Because of brain trauma and lasting nerve damage
If you touched her, her skin crawled.
Eyes dilated permanently when she was held
She would growl, and I would get mauled
I was trying to help when she scratched both my arms
Until I just tossed her outside.
My heart was broken as I glanced out the glass door
And heard her soft, pitiful cry.

I tried a couple names like "Honey" and "Treble"
For my fluffy Siamese pretty,
But none of the names stuck because she was to be
Permanently Baby Kitty.
I took her to the vet for her first feline shots
Also, she needed to be spayed.
Sadly, I left her there and then made arrangements
To come pick her up the next day.

When I picked up Baby, the doctor said, guess what?
She had been neutered, and surprise!
Baby Kitty was a he instead of a she;
With a smile I said my good byes.
When I got home, I tried to learn which parts of him
I could and I should never touch.
As I learned to understand about Baby's pain,
I found I loved him very much.

As the years rolled on by, we became very close
He seemed to never leave my side
My little nerve-damaged fluffy kitty with those
Dilated beautiful blue eyes.
Now you might ask how it's possible to love such
A damaged, most difficult cat
He offered me total unconditional love,
And sometimes he gave more than that.

Through all of his needs, health problems, cortisone shots
And all of his trips to the vet
He always came running at the sound of my voice
And on that I could win a bet
When I rubbed two fingers together, he would come
And even follow me outside
Baby Kitty would never run away from me,
Nor did he ever try to hide.

After ten years, Baby Kitty's kidneys failed
As I cradled him in my arm
The vet eased his pain as Baby looked in my eyes
He trusted I'd keep him from harm.
My little, forever precious Baby Kitty
That went through so much undue pain.
Went to his final rest and I knew in this world
I would never pet him again.

(Continued on next page)

I have cried many, many tears since that sad day
It seems such a long time ago.
I'd never have a pet that close to me again
And this I do certainly know.
Got a card in the mail I'll always remember
From my Baby Kitty's last vet
Thanking me for giving care to Baby Kitty
When other people would have left.

Now, if the truth be known my loveable Baby
Was not really the lucky one.
I'd found the unconditional love I'd always needed
Before my earthly life was done.
Baby gave more than any other animal
That came into my life to love.
I know inside Baby Kitty was sent to me,
As a gift from heaven above.

HANGRY ATTACK

When one has gone beyond hungry
And is bordering on angry
Unfocused and can barely see
We've entered the realm of hangry

Walking dead need something to drink.
Cranky can't concentrate or think.
With nourishment, life does come back
We're saved from the hangry attack!

Creative Leap

Streaming truth outward
With knowledge sharing
Collaborating
Innate thoughts pairing.

What humanity
Has sown, shall it reap
Unless shared thoughts bring
A creative leap.

RHYTHMS OF REALITY

Ideas flowing in many rhythmic patterns
Connecting what was with what's to come
Gathering, storing new truths along the way
While holding on to where we came from.

The pulsing cadence of the biorhythm
Ever moving, ever growing thus
Each pattern spawning a new reality
Creating the life story of us.

TRUE PATH

Way too many years were spent
Seeking what I believed,
Trusting in what I was told,
So easily deceived.

Looking outside of the box,
My spirit eyes could see.
All that I needed to know
Was already in me.

Needed to mature to see
Through intuitive eyes,
Shaving the wheat from the shaft
Of those ritual lies.
Now I know belief systems

Are ropes to hold onto.
It is love that should be shown
In all I say and do.

Truth is my power,
A blooming flower,
Not hatred or wrath.
Love is my true path.

Drawing by Benjamin Mankin

CHANGE, PATIENCE AND TRUTH

A transfigured soldier named Change
Bends with the wind
While the turbulent storm is swirling fast.

A spirit warrior called Patience
Stands still knowing,
Before long, turmoil will be in the past.

An awaiting archer deemed Truth,
When time is right,
Will innovate veracity at last.

ALEX: Wow! Truth is such a big topic, one that touches each one of us every single day. Truth is not absolute, but rather context-sensitive and situation-dependent. This means that truth is relative to the situation at hand, and we are in the center of that situation as the person who is perceiving that truth. What may be true in one situation, may not be true in another situation.

From a human perspective, there are no absolute truths. When a new situation occurs where a concept that was previously considered as truth does not fit, then a larger concept exists that encompasses this new concept, and our job is to find that higher level of truth. Since humans operate from a place of yearning to know the truth, when prompted by insecurity, our mind often does embrace what we perceive as "absolute truths" in an attempt to develop internal stability. This may take the form of a set of rules or beliefs, deference to an external authority, or a repeatable pattern of past events.

But, when we lock onto a truth as absolute, it causes us to separate from a changing world, and hinders our ability to judge and make decisions from an objective viewpoint, not allowing ourselves to expand our consciousness. As Leonard Cooper, a computer guru and musician, adds, an absolute belief "does not allow the continuous and steady development of unconditional love through the acceptance and understanding of ALL things created in the Universe."

No wonder this idea of truth plays an important role in Cindy's verse!

EMERGING SELF

Seeking selfish desires in vain
While avoiding life's fear and pain
The inner man fought
For freedom of thought
Forging roads with new truths to find
Expanding the self-conscious mind

TRUTH

Truth accepted yesterday
May not be truth for today
Learning, oft in constant flux,
Shows truth in a whole new way.

Think about your solid beliefs
A measly few years ago;
Truths may be quite different
Then the ones you used to know.

Working together and open
To ideas and points of view,
Collaborate while searching,
Unearthing truths ever new.

CINDY: The living of life is so full of beauty and chaos, fear and compassion, all entangled in the illusion of reality. It is in this setting that small can be large and large can be small, otherwise known as life.

Reality can change at any moment
For nothing in life ever stays just the same
How we see our-selves, and how others see us,
Is only a grand illusionary game.

POOL FISACO

It was a beautiful warm Indian summer day
At the big house we all lived in on Seyferth Way
From underneath the pool came a humongous bubble;
That was only the beginning of that day's trouble.

A friend grabbed a knife, thinking the bubble should be popped
Grabbing a child, on the coffee table we hopped
My friend ran into the house without closing the door
Water gushed in and filled the family room floor.

The water poured onto the rug and inched up the wall
Surely everyone heard my alarming call
There was so much water that the Apricot tree fell
I'd like to say that's all, but there's still more to tell.

Then inch by inch we dragged that wet rug ever so far
Around the house to dry on the top of the car
Like a period at the end of the day, that's it,
Opening the garage, there was a pile of dog shit!

SOUL FRIEND

Have you ever met someone
You are sure you've met before?
The longer you are with them,
You are drawn in even more.

Seems like they really know you
Everything aligns just right.
You hang on to every word,
Even late into the night.

When it's time to say goodbye
To this intriguing new friend
A feeling hangs over you,
As if this has always been.

I'd venture to say you've seen
A soul friend from days of ole
A shadow from time before,
A family member of the soul.

Live the Music

Flat sixth, flat seventh, lifting the soul
Upward bound, a weaving roll
Shed the puppet strings
See what the music brings
Soar high, clearing the mind
Peering beyond the subconscious blind.

Flat sixth, flat seventh, up octave two
Waking the inner most you
songs of jubilee
Lost in euphony
Bathed in sounds so glorious
Surrendered, meek and victorious.

RHYTHMS

Swirling, whirling sounds from everywhere
Pulling my thoughts, spinning here and there
As the wind through the chattering leaves doth blow
Gives feeling to life's breathing of ebb and flow
Turning of earth sets into motion
Rhythmic waves crashing the bleached ocean.

The warmth of the day's sunrise bringing
Intertwined morning song birds singing
A waterfall's powerful rumbling sound
Mesmerizing patterns of rain hit the ground
A gentle stream's flow, finding its way,
Setting the rhythm for a new day.

Steady cadence of the heart beating
In this compulsive life so fleeting,
Pulsating through veins as the red blood courses
Many sensations call forth new life forces.
Rhythm of converging hearts surges,
A driven pattern from which love emerges.

ALEX: So much music emerged, and then, Cindy had a wonderful collaboration with her children … and they would write and sing together. "All to You Lord" was just such a collaboration.

ALL TO YOU LORD
(Verses and chorus by Robin Hills)

When I fail, when I fall
You are with me through it all
Your love heals and Your mercy saves
Your grace rescued me
And Your blood set us free

I raise my hands up, all for You
I raise my voice Lord, all for You
You hear my cries, heal my pain
Give me strength all my days
I give my life Lord, all to You

When I'm broken and in pain
You are there Lord to break my chains
Your love heals and Your mercy saves
Your grace rescued me
And Your blood set us free

I turn my eyes up, yeah, all to You
I put my trust Lord, all in You
You hear my cries, heal my pain
Give me strength in all my days
I give my life Lord, all to You

REFRAIN:

All to You, all to You
I give my life Lord, all to You
All to You, all to You
I give my life Lord, all to You

Dream

Let my dream be guarded
Discovering pathways to new truths
Casting away all harm
Gathering forever flowing love.

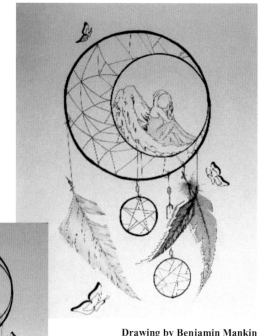

Drawing by Benjamin Mankin

ALL THAT IS ME

To be conscious, to dream
To create, to be
To navigate, to change
To adjust, to see
To become all that is me.

And through all the living, so many, many lessons and so many ideas that pulled verse from my head and heart. So, I made lists. Here's one example.

[I] Children caught in the crossfire of anger become survivalists with stunted growth in becoming the people they were meant to be.

[II] Victim or perpetrator, we've all lived on both sides.

[III] If only looking back when navigating life's roads, then you're not paying attention to where you're going.

[IV] What unfolds in front of me in this life is what I'm meant to see. The roads I've traveled have valuable lessons along the way, with the journey more important than the destination.

[V] Life is not random; all actions have a purpose.

[VI] Whether negative or positive, conscious or unconscious, we are always creating.

[VII] Lessons, stories and experiences storied in fractals help us in our future endeavors. Without these fractals we would cease to mature.

[VIII] A lifetime of seeking love can be lived only to find that love was actually surrounding you the whole time.

[IX] Pain can be intoxicating as well as addictive; hence, luring the soul into remaining a victim. Pain held within is a self-maintained prison of the mind.

[X] Freedom is the ability to live as you choose as long as it does not harm another. Without understanding that freedom we can stunt one another's growth.

[XI] Judgement of others comes from the heart and shows what battles you yourself have yet to overcome.

[XII] Let all that we are stewards of be in our thoughts every day and become an important part of our lives. As a servant to others and the earth, we are given the opportunity to experience and learn, gaining in spiritual growth.

TRUE CHARITY

An instant of astounding
Clarity,
Mesmerizing moment of
Verity,
With humans united in
Parity,
A Soulful heart exudes true
Charity.

GIFTS

See with spiritual eyes
Touch with kindness and mercy
Hear with great understanding
Speak with loving compassion
Create all life can offer.

CINDY: Some people learn quickly, others are slower. I would, unfortunately, frequently take longer than most, and I, of course, living with a heavy dose of OCD, would be totally immersed, sometimes even drowning, in my life lesson. But gradually, I began to see what was going on behind the vale, deep in my unconscious, and began to know—and focus in on—what was really important to me.

Meditation, which brought new clarity to my understanding of the world, became a favorite tool for quieting the monkey chatter that coursed through my head, and opening to higher guidance. This continues to be a tool that I treasure and use still today.

LIFE JOURNEY

Know that each soul is on a journey
Exploring and seeking discernment
While living life lessons and growing
During this brief earthly internment.

Concentrating on what's important
Cultivating a shared mindfulness
Gaining enlightenment while seeking
Ultimately expanding consciousness.

Drawing by Lenore Joans

SUFFERING'S ONLY FOR A SEASON

Suffering's only for a season.
When we've done something wrong,
Why must we always and forever
Play that suffering song?
Let the past be over when we know
We have grown from within.
There's time for reconciliation
And time for healing's end.

So many times we have reached inside
Peeled off the scab to bleed
So healing must start over again.
Pay attention! Take heed!
Many years of mending is needed
When rehashing the past
Learn, grow up, move on, and only then
Will needed healing last.

We are doomed to repeat our mistakes
Again, and then again
'Till we finally figure it out.
Then, repair can begin.
Think about how hard our lives have been
Freedom has to be earned.
Time to get it right, for there are more
Life lessons to be learned.

So, pay your dues and then just move on
No need to tell you how
I am pretty sure that you have it
Well figured out by now
You have suffered enough singing those
Misery songs; for what reason?
You should know by now that suffering's
Only for a Season.

UNSETTLED

When the languishing mind becomes unsettled
A needy heart is involved
Usually there are intrusive emotions
Lingering, to be resolved.
Reaching inside of me to understand those
Unsettled feelings of doubt,
I look around to make sure that I'm truly
Traveling the better route.

Unresolved disturbances seem to keep me
So tightly, desperately bound,
Though I try to ignore them and then pretend
They are really not around.
I just go on with the business of living
With the distractions we share,
Doing things that take me familiar places,
Although I am not sure where.

Trying to figure out just what's going on
Inside this armor of me,
I envelope those deep unsettled feelings
That are not letting me see.
Usually there's a lesson waiting for me,
Though distractions slow me down,
While swimming in the sea of my emotions
Looking for help lest I drown.

Now older, it's harder to keep my perceived
Unshakable state of mind.
The world seems to be moving so much faster
And paths are harder to find.
These lessons I'm continuously learning
Are increasingly showing
How this tired-but-now-liberated soul may
unceasingly keep growing.

CINDY: It took many years to finally free my mind, body and soul of that victim mentality that held me hostage for a good portion of my life. Being the victim was my friend, my enemy and sometimes my savior. Victimhood felt like it was just my lot in life. I had no idea just how much of a hold it had on me. When I finally rid myself of those self-blinders and began to face my demons, I knew that it would not be easy. Hurting those I loved and those closest to me was by far the hardest of my unintentional transgressions to forgive myself for. Asking for forgiveness from others was easier than forgiving myself.

I wrote poetry and prose to express the lessons I now learned but that was not enough. I pulled out the story of me I had started in my twenties and decided I needed to finish it for my family. All I had in my hand was what I could remember hand printed in pencil on lined paper. So, I turned on the computer and with the help of ancestry, began a journey of my mind, body and soul. As I researched Ancestry, the story of the family I knew little about came slowly, piece by piece.

When I began to write about myself without realizing it, I was laying down each burden as I lived through my emotions, story after story. It was as if I was there again as an observer feeling everything. I've been told I was like a gentle fluffy bunny in a hurricane, and indeed I was that naive! It is my hope that my children will learn from my experiences by bringing my life story into the light and casting those skeletons out of the closet one by one.

It took a couple of years, but with the help and encouragement of my sister (found on Ancestry, story shared later in this book), it was finally finished. What I did not see coming was how I was released—mind, body and soul—when the book was done. What an epic surrender! I had relived my life and was no longer a victim. I had become an observer of all those life lessons! I could now see the whole path instead of just portions.

I now know that everything happened just as it should have, for this is what makes me who I am today.

MADE ME WHO I AM TODAY

If you ask how I got through the confusion
Of those down and out days in my life,
I used to say I'd chosen the wrong road,
I wanted a shorter road with less strife.

I would then pick another door to go through
Without asking the big question: Why?
I'd head one direction, and when that was wrong,
I'd just fall down on my knees and cry

I began to look around on my journeys,
Not just focused on the life-long run
I was less afraid and began to embrace
Each obstacle till each test was done.

I realized it wasn't the path I'd chosen.
These were lessons I needed to learn
That kept me meandering around detours,
Each dead end, and unexpected turn.

Those irrational fears I'd carried with me
Kept me stagnant in spiritual growth,
Fear of being alone and of the unknown,
Clearly, I needed to conquer both.

Looking back, I'm asking, would I change anything?
After all is done, here's what I say:
Everything happened just as it should have, and
That's what made me who I am today!

ALEX: Yes. "Made Me Who I Am Today" resonates with the research we've done here at the Mountain Quest Institute. During the course of life, we all face negative and positive experiences, sometimes of our own making and other times emerging out of seemingly nowhere. Regardless of the origins of these events, our emotional, mental and physical responses—whether conscious or unconscious—are our own.

Threatening or anxiety-provoking events play a role in our growth and expansion. As Cindy often weaves throughout her work, every event in life, no matter how traumatic, can provide some aspect of learning. For example, if you have learned nothing else, you have learned that you do not choose to have this event repeat itself. While certainly difficult to do while in the midst of a negative experience, as you move further away from the event and process the subjective memory in a variety of ways, you can begin to *reflect on it from a systems viewpoint* as a learning lesson. Then, over time, you can begin to appreciate the value of this lesson, and with that appreciation comes the realization that this lesson from the past has contributed to who you are today. You can potentially reach a point of gratitude, that is, actually being thankful for the learning experience.

The word gratitude has Latin roots from *gratus*, meaning pleasing or thankful, and *gratia*, meaning favor or thanks, and in Spanish and French it translates as *gracia*. When used as a name, made popular by 17th-century Puritans, Gracia means "inspired by grace", with grace representing beauty, kindness and mercy.

Mercy gleaned from learning forgiveness

Teaching the heart unconditional love

Giving honor and dignity to others

Birthing kindness, reveal beauty,

Bestowing grace to the living soul.

ALEX: When we move through experiences to the point of being grateful for them, the negative emotional tag related to the experience has become less and less prominent, diminishing altogether as the event is perceived as a positive learning experience, occupying a place in objective memory (follow track #2 in the figure below). As new learning lessons emerge and take center stage in terms of focus, the event may disappear entirely from memory, although the lesson as a pattern remains available as needed.

This, of course, describes the ideal outcome for a threatening or anxiety-provoking event. And, indeed, when we take ownership of this process, working through awareness, understanding, belief, and feeling good about our learning—and have enough knowledge and confidence to apply that learning—we have the ability to successfully do so. However, deep emotions can be difficult to deal with. For example, an event can be so deeply embedded (track #1 in the figure below) that you are in a state of denial regarding the importance or impact of the event. Conversely, you could be so caught up in reliving the event over and over again that there isn't any space to separate from the event and reflect (track #3 in the figure below).

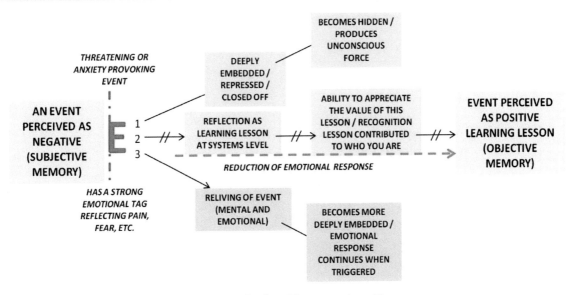

Learning Cycle for Threatening Events

REFLECTING MIRRORS

Traveling through life, glimpses of the truth
Were occasionally shown to me
Somewhat like frantically treading water
While desperately struggling to see.
Forever kicking and reaching upward
Searching for the distant secure shore
It was not easy to see what was there
A raging thirst left me wanting more.

Even though gleaning inspired impressions
Of the things that I needed to learn,
I could not yet completely understand
The teachings I needed to discern.
Then along comes another life lesson
Sending me another direction
I get distracted and lost in my thoughts
Then miss another life reflection.

Someone who was very close decided
They would show me where I had gone wrong
Propelling the truth right up to my face
Sounding an ever-repeating song.
I turned away quite overwhelmed with fear
Feeling judgment, my emotions gushed,
A deep anger seething inside of me,
All that I believed I was, now crushed.

My intimidated heart over-filled
With an intensified piercing pain,
Feeling the lecture that I was hearing
With nothing in it for me to gain.
My wounded spirit bulldozed the door shut
Protecting all that was left inside
From the person holding the mirror
And from my own self I chose to hide.

There is one clear truth that I know for sure
And that person needs to understand
Do not hold up those Reflecting Mirrors
Not knowing what the heart can withstand.
Not family, friends or acquaintances
Nor complete strangers, nor even me,
Can forward mirrored truths that will prevail
Till a person is ready to see.

Now, can you tell me what was the purpose
Of looking at the things that I've done
When you have growing you must do yourself
And have countless battles to be won?
Reflecting mirrors can damage the soul
When a person's not ready to grow
Take heed when you choose to judge others
Through "Reflecting Mirrors of the Soul".

ALEX: The innate ability to evoke meaning through understanding and comprehension—to evaluate, judge and decide—distinguishes the human mind from most other life forms. There is an element of judging in every decision we make. In fact, judging is used far more than logic or rational thinking in making decisions!

However, Cindy's poem is focused specifically on judging others. The act of judging others and their actions requires something or someone to judge against. When one individual is judging another person, it is in the context of a scale, with the individual who is judging generally located somewhere in the middle of that scale. If the individual that is judging is egotistical, arrogant or insecure with themselves, there may be a need to judge others as less in order to prove personal superiority or (artificially) feel better about oneself. Alternately, if an individual's self-regard is low, an individual may judge others above themselves, which will prove or justify one's feelings and add to one's insecurity. Thus, we discover that when we are judging others, we are defining ourselves.

Often, the people we are judging are showing us *a part of ourselves that we do not like*, or that they are comfortable with *things we are unable to do or that we dislike in ourselves.* As we mature and learn who we are, the judging of others gives way to awareness and discernment, that is, in our interactions it is no longer necessary to contrast others on our personal scale, while still important to the knowing of who they are (values, beliefs, etc.) Discernment is perception; judgment is criticism.

JUDGEMENT & COMPASSION

Why do we easily judge one another,
Not thinking about the damage we inflict,
Assuming that we know what's best for others
Without even trying to walk in their shoes.
Why do our judged actions seem so offensive
To our shallow blinded eyes and emotions?
Could it be we've not yet fully forgiven
Those particular offenses in our self?

Lessons learned in life continually migrate
From awakening to discerning compassion
Through the forgiving of others and ourselves,
Asking forgiveness for harm that we have done.
Only then can we grasp what it would be like
To be caught in another's perceived prison.
When we don't work through all the pain and suffering,
Then the lack of forgiveness leads to judgement.

Accusations and judging are overcome
Through understanding, mercy and compassion,
Rising above the sea of man's transgressions
Bringing strong turbulence to the reposed state.
We can learn how to uplift one another
With love, both physically and spiritually,
Being tolerant as we walk unique paths
In this awakening of spiritual growth.

RAIN JUST FALLS

Sometimes it's hard watching life transpire
Why do the kindhearted get burned by fire?
We're taught that all things work for the good
If I could take your place, I gladly would.

This world is filled with famine and blight
At times it can seem hard to find the light
Storms continue to rage as they must
The rain falls on both the just and unjust.

GROWING

Now, just embrace your time of life pain,
For what else is there to do?
When wondering if this life is sane,
Well, it's just all up to you.

You could just run and hide from yourself,
Spending life in the same place,
Seeking alluring power and wealth,
Running a selfish life race.

But for all those who refuse to learn,
This fleeting life does not last.
The life-long lessons they do not earn
Shall again repeat the past.

LOOKING FOR UGLY

When judging, we think we're focusing on
Someone's iniquities
Verily, bringing into the light our own
Unseen obliquities
Seems easy to see other's wrongdoings,
So called impurities
While we're actually peering through a lens
Of insecurities
A deluded human self-esteem builder,
Acting rather smugly,
Often finds much more than was bargained for
When looking for ugly.

Hope Eternal

From the lips, kind words spoken
To a tender heart broken,
Ushering in hope eternal,
Fervid light ever vernal.

DUST IN THE WIND

If you do not share your thoughts and memories
When you pass on, do they die too?
What was the reason for all that you've learned
If you take those lessons with you?

There is that story about your parents
And the sacrifices they made
Passed through a life-time from parent to child
As memories that all too soon fade.

When children wonder about who they are,
Contemplating where they come from,
What a blessing if they could see or hear
A few words that could enrich life's outcome.

And if those memories and lessons vanish
When we come to our journey's end
All those life experiences will be lost,
Becoming just "Dust in the Wind".

V. Healing Deep Wounds

YOUNG DREAMER

Young dreamer, living life so impetuous
Wearing those blinders can make life perilous
Thinking what you are seeing is marvelous
Yet all that surrounds you is quite nebulous

Being drawn to the unknown ambiguous
Naivety believes in one so credulous
And showing such a need to be emulous
Time to open your eyes to the frivolous

One day this dreamer won't be so impetuous

LIFE BLINDERS ON

Life Blinders on my eyes
Mournful cries
Won't take long
Soon, something else goes wrong

THIS TOO SHALL PASS

Every time something goes wrong in life,
Do you wonder what to do?
Do you contemplate, how in the world
Will you ever make it through?

After considering all the options
And the problems from the past,
Try to stay calm and say to yourself,
You know that *this too shall pass.*

Does it seem that in times of crisis
All you want to do is cry?
Remind yourself, it's time to move on,
For every low has its high.

Now you might think that perseverance
Is the answer, but, alas,
Life is so precious and very short.
Believe me, *this too shall pass*!

CINDY: And so, life goes on: up/down, laughing/crying, learning/blind, and so forth, experiencing all the dualities that define our boundaries and understanding. While many moments of discord have been shared, there are four focused areas that reflect deep wounds of the heart and mind. While all the events of our life are different—for we are each unique in our learning journeys—many of the thoughts and feelings may represent your personal experiences. We all have skeletons in the closet waiting to be acknowledged and purged. Let's take off the blinders and take a closer look.

SKELETONS IN THE CLOSET

Everyone has skeletons in the closet
That they think are gone and out of sight.
But clearly, nothing stays hidden forever
Though we can always hope that it might.
And even if no one else ever finds out,
When at end of life we face ourselves
Do not be deluded thinking you've hidden
Those thoughts and desires on closet shelves.

Giving into our hormones often brings us
To pulsating, compulsive desire
We discover ourselves dabbling, then drowning
In all of living's muck and quagmire.
We look away, declaring it just can't be,
So deep-seeded in the heart of man,
It's the flesh we're actually warring against,
Trying to outsmart it when we can.

There's another way to face the ugliness
Of deep-rooted harmful thoughts and acts
Bringing them to the radiant, cleansing light
Which tempers hidden desires and facts.
The spirit opens a pathway for cleansing
Burdens of the heart left unshaken
Before that last account of our thoughts and deeds
Are uncovered when we awaken.

We battle with good and evil every day
In everything we say and we do
Sifting wheat from the shaft is a lifetime job
That is happening in me and you.
Just thinking we have somehow managed to change
Doesn't hide those skeletons away.
It's cleansing light that burns away the poison
From our hearts and our souls every day.

Drawing by Benjamin Mankin

Piety is another grand toxin that binds
Keeping us from freedom of the soul
It motivates us to hurt one another
Without thought, if I may be so bold.
Even those who will claim to have the answer
Can sometimes do a lot of damage.
We need to take inventory of our life
Which each one of us needs to manage.

As to Judgment, you see, on this earth no one
Is really better than the other.
Each one can lift up the other in kindness,
Whether friend, foe, sister or brother.
It's not through criticism and preaching
Nor with our own judgements we should sit
For all humans that walk upon this great earth
*Have their **Skeletons in the Closet**.*

Abuse

INNOCENCE LOST

Innocence lost, taken long before time
Leaves the little lamb anything but fine
Who can this child turn to for affection?
Virtue robbed through a perceived infection.

Lost beseech soul who is doomed not to bloom
Life's transformation came along too soon
Naively looking at life through child eyes
Damaged inside, no one hears the still cries.

It takes many years to silence the pain
Through alcohol, drugs and acting insane
She'll travel countless roads till she can see
The guilt was not hers, and that sets her free!

CINDY: Abuse comes in many forms—physical, mental and emotional—and is often difficult to identify for those who have no frame of reference other than fear and pain, all of which are based on the belief that they are bad, that this is their fault, that they deserve it. And, oh, it takes so very long to understand that **this is not the truth**. I guess that's why truth is so important in the verse that continues to sing out in my head and heart.

I sang songs inside and made up stories that were never voiced. I was unable to function in school or other social settings, and after much testing and counseling, retaining my silence and despite a high IQ when tested, I was labeled as "emotionally retarded." I would suggest I was traumatized.

BIRTHDAY UNDER A BUSH

Still here, not understanding why
So very sad, can't even cry
No longer know where I belong
Everything in life feels wrong.

Squeezed in tight like a human wedge
Memories tucked in under the hedge
From myself I'm trying to hide
In this lonely backyard, outside.

Birthday fourteen, for goodness sake
Even made my own birthday cake
Yard's so quiet and no one's about
No songs, no candles to blow out.

Can this bush and I become one?
In this hedge, gazing at the sun
Oh, living leaves somewhat shading
All too soon just a memory fading.

Frozen birthday moment in time
Soon this home no longer is mine
Never to belong here evermore
Pushing through that revolving door!

FATHERLESS CHILD

Looking back on my life there were many times
I thought for sure that I was alone.
But somehow most things managed to be alright;
That's really something I should have known.
It did seem like someone, or maybe some thing,
Was always there looking out for me.
When all is said and done, it just comes down to:
It was simple, but I could not see.

It does seem as if I went through life
With one problem after another.
I am sure I wasn't a good example
For either my sister or brother.
Every time I would fall down, flat on my face,
Someone was right there picking me up.
Do you think someone was watching over me,
Or maybe it was just plain dumb luck?

Looking back at all of my so-called problems
That apparently worked themselves out,
The idea of someone watching over me
Now to me is no longer in doubt.
Pondering long on the father I never had,
I finally understood and smiled
I was contented in the concept that "He"
Watches over His "Fatherless Child".

CINDY: Finally, in 2016, I began searching again for my father, siblings, and any family I could find, including cousins, etc. I would have been very happy just to find any relatives at all, and was pleased to see that there was so much more information on the Internet now than the last time I had searched. Momma had never told me the names of any relatives of mine either on my father's side or her side of the family, except Uncle Bob Jenkins, who she really liked.

So, it was time to try again after giving up the search in 2006, when all I had found was a name which looked like it might be my father. However, the ancestry document claimed that the Cleo Bernard Scott that I'd found did not have any children. Yet it was the only Cleo Bernard Scott of the correct age and birthplace that could possibly be him! Oh, well. During that same search period, I also checked with an agency and put my name on a compiled data bank that was for children looking for birth parents or siblings. When nothing showed up, I just figured that maybe that was just the way it was going to be. So, I put it all on the back burner and out of my mind.

ALEX: Cindy had the opportunity, and sometimes the heartbreak, of having our birth mother come in and out of her life as she grew toward maturity. All along, Cindy knew there were others before her, and, more clearly, remembered there had been a little brother after her. Yet her mother, who when she was around would cry herself to sleep every night, never broached the subject, such that Cindy pretended, for the most part, that she did not remember, that she did not know. Yet, as an adult, and particularly after building a relationship with a full sibling in the latter years, she often reflected on the pain her mother carried: A continuing relationship with a man who had another family, accented by periodic abandonment. Rejection by her family. Five children born out of wedlock. No means of developing a livelihood.

In those times, in this place, she perceived no choice, and yet made a hard choice, holding onto that choice throughout a lifetime of silence. Cindy's "Never Meant to Be" captures the pain of this choice.

NEVER MEANT TO BE

Born out of love, and never meant to be
Steeped in betrayal it's all she could see
Denied by blood, left with children of love
No help coming, from below or above.

How can she live and survive without him?
With blameless sweet children born into sin
Nowhere to turn and her world upside down
A heart wrenching pain, with no one around.

What can she do with everything wrong?
Needs to be met and funds won't last long
How can she choose which ones to let go?
A lifetime of sadness she will soon know.

Tears will fall silent as time moves on by
While inside she's throbbing and sobbing: **Why?**
The soul's pain is dulled by the sting of death
In quiet strength the secret breathes its last breath.

After retirement and while living with my fourth child, my sweet Becky and my baby grandchild Sebastian, I had extra time on my hands. So, I decided to try again and see if I could find some family. One more time, I began a journey of gathering information, but this time I put much more effort into the details.

First, I decided to send off for a better copy of my birth certificate. The copy I had was very old (from when I was a child), was blackened from age, and could barely be read. When I received the new certified copy of my birth certificate, I was amazed at how much information there was for me to glean off just that one document. For example, my name was misspelled ... hmmm ... and my father's age at my birth was now visible, among other small but important facts, such as affirming that I was the fourth child of this union. This made sense. One of my brothers was older than me, and there were two older sisters.

Another piece of invaluable information was in a letter from my mother I found in my memory trunk. After I found it, I remembered getting that letter, and was filled with renewed vigor and challenge for the hunt. In that letter from my mother was information about my father's death. He had died in the summer of 1986, and my mother went on to explain how to find out where the Scott family lived by writing to White Sulfur Springs, Greenbrier, West Virginia, and addressing it to the Scott clan. After reading that old letter, I remembered getting a phone call from my mother telling me to write to my father's home town and address it to the Scotts if I ever choose to get in touch with them. I had small children at the time, so I just put the information away for another time (hence, the memory trunk). I'm not sure why my mother finally gave me that bit of information, but I'm sure glad I held on to that letter!

I began building a family tree through ancestry.com and also, one at a time, had DNA done on all my immediate family members that would participate. I was very pleased how much the Internet had progressed over the years since my first search. Every day I would check for new information on either Cleo Bernard Scott or Nettie Rae Jenkins (Peggy). I even guessed at the names of my siblings, of which only one name I knew for sure. I had also talked at length with my stepfather before he passed, and he told me that he was present with my mother in court in Washington, DC, when she signed the final papers for the boy's adoptions. That would have been around 1950. So, another piece of the puzzle was in place, or at least I hoped that was the case!

I had so many questions, and little did I know then that they were about to be answered in a large way.

NATURE VERSUS NURTURE

Five sibling souls predestined by a parent's promise
That all five of them would never meet,
Although choosing to spend a lifetime with each other
With lessons and powers to defeat.

All were separated and given to new parents,
Who adopted them to be their own.
They were never meant to discover one another;
Out of five, two are still left unknown.

What if we had been brought up together as siblings,
Which the five of us could (should) have been?
Would we still have lived these predestined life journeys
If we had stayed a family back then?

Now, this brings up a very interesting discussion
On how nature works versus nurture.
We all grew up not knowing about one another,
Our common traits, intriguing for sure.

If we do choose our lineage before we are born
And life's choices are not just by chance,
Are our lives somehow guided to learn the same lessons,
No matter the age or circumstance?

This brings up a fascinating question, how much life
Is really our own freedom of choice?
I think it all just depends on how long it takes us
To listen to our inner voice.

This seriously brings doubt to the well-liked theory
That life is just random acts of chance.
That in an instinctive world we live void of insight,
Marching along in a mortal trance.

Why else would we live our lives with this glorious gift
Of awareness, from our birth to death?
Except to learn from life lessons about creation
Until we draw our very last breath.

In March of 2016, while doing a routine search on Cleo Bernard Scott and Nettie Rae Jenkins, a new document showed up on Nettie Rae Scott, which would have been her name if she had been married. This was a shift from scouring through pointless leads. The ancestry profile was connected to Cleo B. Scott, and the ancestry profile on Nettie Rae claimed that she had died in 1947, which would have been before I was born in 1948! The bad news is that she was also connected to a child, Cleo Barbara Scott, who was deceased. I had prayed to find one of my siblings, but had wanted to find them alive. One down.

MOMMY, I LOVE YOU

A lifetime of pain she spent wondering
Why her mother had given her away;
The mommy that took her in to love her
Never really knew what to do or say.

The young child grew up feeling abandoned,
Pushing rejection feelings deep within.
Unthoughtful words spoken without wisdom
Tore a rift, with battles no one could win.

A lifetime of searching for missing love
Brought no relief from the deep pain inside.
Through so many failed relationships,
From the truth her tortured soul did hide.

Once again, she became a childlike soul
When an aneurysm released the mind.
No longer able to care for herself,
The mommy fed her and cleaned her behind.

She was cared for through her very last days,
With the mommy doing all she could do.
Looking up with a smile and child-like eyes,
She tenderly said, "Mommy, I Love You".

Finally found peace.
In memory of Cleo Barbara (1946-2006)

Still, I was excited that I had found some kind of information on Nettie Rae and Cleo Barbara, and quickly sent an email to the ancestry preparer explaining who I was, asking her how she came to enter this information, and giving who the correct death date for my mother, Nettie Rae. I also gave the preparer my personal email.

Evidently, she forwarded it to another person who had been involved in the process. I was surprised when I received such a quick response from an "Alex", an unknown name to me at the time. The email was short, but as I read, it was from Cleo Barbara's younger sister! I couldn't believe it! I had a sister alive, and had her name, which was nothing close to her birth name which was Martha Ellen! I immediately called each one of my children to tell them the news.

My youngest child and her husband (Mike and Robin) got on the line, and found a picture of Alex, my sister, on Facebook. I remember Robin's excited voice laughing and saying, "Mom she looks like you with short hair!" There was no doubt in Robin's mind that this was indeed my sister!

I got on Facebook and found the Mountain Quest Institute, and there she was with her husband. I could not even contain the unbelievable, overwhelming emotions coming over and through me! With my body running somewhere between nervous and excitement, I called the Inn. Alex was not there; she was out running errands. I left my phone number with the message that I thought that we might be sisters ... and patiently waited for a return call.

EMERGING MELODY

Two siblings, unknown separation,
Found each other with jubilation.
Divergent walks are now converging;
A symphony is now emerging.

As the new melody does unfold,
Truth becomes new music to the soul.
Knowing each other was meant to be
Lost-then-found sisters' spirits set free.

FIRST CONTACT

I remember looking over the Mountain Quest pictures and gazing at what was supposed to be my sister. It just all seemed so unbelievable. Could it really be true? After almost sixty-eight years, had we really found one another? It was, really, the unimaginable imagined forming into reality! Had I really found one of my siblings? My excitement was through the roof!

I wasn't sure how Alex would feel about talking to a sister ... Did she even *know* she had a younger sister? [The answer was "no".] Was I intruding on her life, like my Mother feared might happen? Would she receive me kindly, or would I seem intrusive to her?

That phone call finally came. On the other end of the line was a kind and strangely familiar voice that said, "So I hear you may be my sister?" I nervously laughed and said, "I think so." This is the beginning of a new story in both of our lives ... What I have learned, and do know, is that everything happens exactly as it should, for that is what makes us who we are today!!!!!!!

NO LONGER ALONE

Alone through life, so I thought
Searching for the love I sought
Looking at the world eyes wide,
Angels serving as my guide.

Winding life up near the end
Found a sister and a friend.
Someone very much like me,
Who was always meant to be.

At times, hand in hand walking,
Sometimes unspoken talking.
Life's work now becoming clear
Out of a love so sincere.

SISTERS

When I feel your strong spirit
Reaching out to mine
Our life force for just a while
Becomes intertwined.

Seeking a familiar place
Where you talk with me
We share segments of our lives
That others can't see.

You open an inner door
And invite me in
We embrace in the spirit
Sharing where we've been.

In that inner room we meet
Knowing each other
Sharing special gifts we've
honed
With one another.

As I shared my life with you
You encounter me
Together, we know things are
just as they should be.

THE GATHERING

Arriving from two thousand
Seven hundred miles away
Excitement hanging in the air
On this beautiful day
We come from many different places
Over land and by sea
At last, the moment arrived
That was never meant to be.

With open arms and warm hearts
Reaching for their first embrace
Cousins, brother, sisters, and aunts
Met at Mountain-Quest place
Familiar feelings, happy smiles,
Eyes filled with swelling tears
Truth finally saw the light
After so many long years.

And in this new beginning
We discover more of us
We laugh and share our closest thoughts
And joke and tease and fuss
And quite suddenly we realize,
While discovering "we",
Perhaps it is the timing
That was always meant to be.

Disease and Aging

SLOW PROGRESSION

I did not feel quite so alone
When I still moved around on my own
I'd visit family or a friend
Now difficult, that came to an end.

In each of this disease's stages
Fear consumes me while the pain rages
Surviving PD's progression
Brings me to a state of confession.

It is sobering for me to see
I can't control what's happening to me.

LIFE IN FLUX

Waking up each day, there is a journey I'd like to share
I sit up while pondering the trek to my bedroom chair
But the restroom is the first place that's calling me, you see
Leaning on two standing canes, an instancy avails me.

Greatly struggling to get there so I don't make a mess
That sense of urgency brings forth a feeling of distress
Upon completion of my task, it's time to put on clothes
In a basket there are garments that I'd already chose.

Steps toward the bed from the bathroom are maybe five or six
Then I slowly sort of make the bed, using a few tricks
Rolling into bed, I pull the covers up to the top
I straighten them the best I can, then giving up, I stop.

KEEP ON KEEPING ON

Now getting old

Wisdom is like gold

Getting beat down

Just act like a clown.

When getting stuck

Try to not give up.

Under attack,

Try to stay on track.

Life's a marathon

We've all undergone

So, sing a song:

Keep On Keeping On!

.... **An eon gone.**

CINDY: "Hang on!" became my battle cry. And, sure enough, at least so far in life, the hanging on brought me to a better place (accompanied by the help of various medications when it's really tough). Intermingled with these painful events was the writing, and sure enough, "hang on" crept into the verse!

Hanging On

These arms and legs, they will not move
I would, I could, I must prove
Constricting toes and burning feet
Self, do not declare defeat!

Hanging on tight 'til all is well
Waves of twitching muscles swell
Trying to ride above the pain
Escalating in the brain.

Sensing your touch until I'm fine
Your strong will engaged with mine
Feeling comforted when you're near
I then realize, "I'm still here."

Caregivers,
Thank you for your selfless love.

DYSKINESIA

Maintaining while the rocking
Takes on its toll,
Staying calm inside when all is
Out of control.
The more that I push back the
Worse it becomes,
With involuntary twitching
Playing air drums.

I try to hang on for as long
As it will last,
Wishing I could cover myself
With a face mask.
Sometimes people murmur it just
Doesn't seem fair,
But I know each of us has our
Own cross to bear.

SLEEP RELIEF

Clenching teeth with a silent shout
Inner explosions that need to get out
Parched lips, rolling tongue, grinding teeth
Rocking back and forth gives little relief.

Curling toes with burning cramped feet
Standing up taking small steps to my seat
Doesn't help, so back to my bed
Trying to control all that's in my head.

Behind the pain, in the dark deep
Searching, waiting, yearning for needed sleep
Leaving the wretchedness behind
And the torture contained in my mind.

For an hour or two, maybe three
Living in a dream, I will gently be
Relief from this worn body's pain
A short existence on a different plane.

Today's a better day.

THE GARDEN OF DEMOCRACY

Corrupted seeds are covered up and left to grow
As the time passes, have no doubt,
Covered seeds eventually sprout
And before long, deep rooted weeds begin to show.

Many years of bad seeds birth freedom's corruption
Fertilized with a selfish greed
Watered by insatiable need
Choked out Democracy brought on an eruption.

Age of transparency becomes the detective
Frustrations caused a great shaking
Impervious eyes are waking
Leading to an open government directive.

Visibility shines light on hypocrisy
Where the covered-up weeds took root
People marching toward truth pursuit
Hoeing weeds in the Garden of Democracy.

Drawing by Kathy Carlisle

SEEKING …

The long-dreaded beast enters in
Through an unguarded gate
Fed by hearts inflamed
Hate breeds hate.

Eyes see what's presumably right
Listening to what they're told
Leading sheep awry
Hearts turn cold

Darkness reigns, growing in power
Sweeping over the land
Infecting sickness
Man to man.

Man reaches out in confusion
Searching for all that's true
Gleaning, learning from
Me and you

A light pierces the confusion
Discerning all that's right
Cleansing contagion
Gaining sight

Only together
with all of our differences
can Democracy survive …

Just a Thought

Does the light burn away the darkness deep?
Or does the dark black hole swallow the light?
In this world where so many souls still sleep
It's time to awaken our visionary sight!

TIME BEFORE CHRISTMAS

It was a time before Christmas and all through the house
Elephants and Donkeys were scurrying about
A statement right here, while over there a shout
Words fired with intensity that no one could douse!

Divergent opinions, everyone making a point
Clashing voices mingled and confusion rang
As the gavel flew through the air with a bang
Left all a wondering, what's happening in this joint?

The Elephants and Donkeys find their whole world shaken
We came down this rabbit hole they so beseeched
Some cry "it's not fair" that our king gets impeached,
As the people's eyes began to awaken.

While we watch the fall of a political steeple
With intense growing pains felt throughout the land
Even with our differences, do *understand*,
This land belongs to a <u>united</u> "We the People"!

WHAT IF?

World Wide Democracy

What if all Earth's people were a world democracy,
With all lands weeded of self-serving plutocracy
Where the greedy and wealthy have no authority,
And this earth is run by a selfless majority?

I must be dreaming again.

Hear the Babies Cry

Can you hear the babies cry?
Where is mommy?
Weeping children don't understand why.

Little ones now frozen in time
Where is daddy?
Lost in a paperwork paradigm.

As time passes, hearts grow cold
Who will love me?
Deep inside the silent tears take hold.

Who will pay for all this pain?
Memories fading,
Hearts are pierced with a permanent stain.

CINDY: How could we as a society let this happen? Have we lost our minds AND our humanity? Why did we not hear? Why did we turn away? Will someone stand up and shine the light on the worst of mankind? The sound of crying babies echoes throughout the nation.

CLARITY OF THOUGHT

In time of crises when there is so much confusion
A calm mind needs to be focused, aware and clear
While others seem frozen in a flight or fight mode
The need to solve the predicament supersedes fear.

Adrenaline overrides fear and ensuing pain
When a situation seems near impossible
Clear thoughts make a conundrum easier to solve
So one can create solutions that are plausible.

University of Life

Growing through life education
With soul orientation
In service learning to cooperate
Uniting all to collaborate.

Together we are co-solving
Learning and co-evolving
Coming together in world unity
Becoming an Earth community.

One by one, each one awaking
Through resolve, co-creating
Spreading altruistic purposefulness
Rising to a higher consciousness.

PEACE

To be correct, or just get along
Endless confusion reigns, who's right and who's wrong?
Go along with what is being shown
Or follow your own path, seemingly alone?

A divided people politicize
Pandemonium rules, humans polarize
Family, strangers, whether foe or friend,
Tell me who is in charge, and when it will end?

The world seems so very different now
Navigating through this human mess, somehow
Dredging bewildered asperity
Seeking love and kindness, peace and charity.

A really pivotal place to start
Is with the condition of the human heart
Within our diversity we must find
A United States with a united mind.

ONE NATION

```
        R
P   E   A   C   E
    S   O
    P   M
    E   P       K
    C H A R I   T Y
    T   S       N
        S       D
        I       N
    L   O V     E
        N       S
                S
```

Build Back Better

UNFOLDING TRUTH

Divisions, past debts, spiritual penetration
Awakening is now upon this generation
While some men are polarized to politicize
Scholars, musicians, poets, and artists prophesize.

People taking to the streets form a new sequel
Chanting epoch aphorisms all are born equal
Young, old, the many hues and nationalities
Unbinding the truths beneath man's inequalities.

We cannot look away and blindly disconnect
Straddling the unscathed fence of voiceless circumspect
While controlling powers and principalities
Catapult oppressive pain with high fatalities.

Hand in hand empowered with love and charity
Our nation is birthing a kindred parity
Watching, listening, the world is waiting to see
If imminent unfolding truths set her people free.

CHOOSE LIFE

Do we seek domination,
A self-serving elaboration,
Or man's emancipation
Through altruistic cooperation?

Join together our resolve;
With diversity we co-evolve.
Through an earth-wide unity
We become a World Community.

And There's Still More ...

VULNERABLE

Virus provisioning
A new envisioning
Who's in control?
Cry's my burdened soul.

Elderly undermined
Shortened lives now defined
Don't understand why
Hear the children cry!

Anger, pain, vanity
Looming insanity
Lying and deceit
Bringing on defeat.

Vulnerability
Our Inability
We can endeavor
When all together.

Our world is anything but fine,
Losing loved ones before their time.

CINDY: And I'm still questioning. What happened? Am I in the wrong country? Have we been asleep? There was a time when I would have been marching in the streets against what is happening in our government, but now I am in my seventies with Parkinson's, and my body will not let me.

It is so infuriating!! All I have left is what I can put into my words on the written page ...

EMPTY PLACE

Arms folded with an unfulfilled embrace
Sadness rolls like waves over this withered face
Looking for meaning in this emptiness
Waiting, hanging on this viral precipice.

Relentless virus moves over the land
Gripping old and weak with the sweep of a hand
The strong try protecting, to no avail,
While the storm just rages, full with rain and hail.

A generation filled with hope so bright
Now facing an unseen, unknown viral blight
It's all depending on, who would've known?
Protection comes in what form? *Being alone.*

Am I safe cradled in this lonely room?
Staring at the four walls, it feels like a tomb
While we're fighting back, when all's said and done,
Death's calling home the love children of the sun.

BACKYARD THOUGHTS

The empty backyard used to seem so big
Now it is looking rather small
Out front I would sit in a rocking chair
Now I don't go out there at all.

So much has changed for us in these
        past months
Will our lives be the same again?
My sad heart aches inside for my family,
With rare visits since it began

The days and nights blur, it all seems the same.
How'd this happen in just one year?
The elderly living everyday lives
Now hiding, surviving in fear.

Multitudes of things we took for granted
Now our lives we must rearrange
Little things I thought would always be there
Oh! How quickly our lives can change.

When taking inventory of the self,
Hanging on the end of our rope,
I now look towards a different future
One filled with empathy and hope.

WORLD WAR V

Behold World War V
The great adaptation
Enemy to all
Every race and nation.

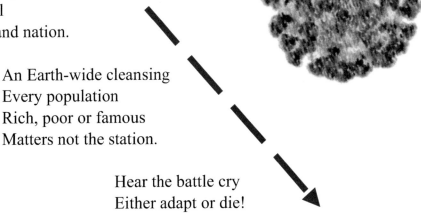

    An Earth-wide cleansing
    Every population
    Rich, poor or famous
    Matters not the station.

        Hear the battle cry
        Either adapt or die!

*With pandemics taking such a hold on life on Earth, it leaves me wondering,
"Will we go down with a battle cry or with a whimper?"*

WEAPON OF MASS DESTRUCTION

The Internet, now available to all
Appears a conduit to mankind's downfall
Reverberating on each domain's station
Skewed while displayed to people in each nation
Giving way to cultish nationalisms
While spawning waves of sensationalisms
People's frustrations are consistently fed
With all the propaganda that's being read.

Political agendas appear the guide
While a multitude of eyes are open wide
Instantaneous judgment assailable
Common sense and reason's not available
Destroying minds and tainting the public thought
Taking the freedoms our visionaries sought
One man's right seems to be another man's wrong
We as earth's stewards must learn to get along!

Wake Up. See the bigger picture.
Oh, vacuous sleep!

WEAPON OF NEW AWAKENINGS

The Internet, which is available to most
Could be mankind's needed collaborative host
Helping many nations, finding new directions
By countries engaging in collaborations
The becoming tolerant of each other's ways
Helps bring calm to these troubling turbulent days
Never before in time could the multitudes see
Information available to you and me.

Now is the time for mankind to become aware
And find a way to solve problems, which all can share
Instantaneous learning is available
To share at the Internet's banqueting table
Bringing all people to a new realization
Each land, province, country, state and every nation
We can start solving problems at each world event
Through a world collaborative entanglement.

Come together and grow.
Our children's future depends on it!

TWENTY-TWENTY

Strategically beseeched
Planned derailment
Nonfeasance to impeach.

In comes COVID nineteen
Invokes lock down
Blindsided, unforeseen.

Hear realities, lies
Some improvised
Observe social demise.

Accusations, Fake News
Information
Colored with many hews.

Strong ideas collided
Voiced, you find
A people divided.

Racism systemic
Integrated
With rabid pandemic.

Thousands take to the streets
"Black Lives Matter"
Years pass, many defeats.

Diversity protest
Kindness abounds
We will not acquiesce.

Will the children be lost?
Emptied out schools
Abandoned at what cost?

It's my right not to mask!
Claustrophobic
What a cumbersome task?

Distancing, we should stay
Scientists beg
At least six feet away.

Try to protect others
For we are all
Soul sisters and brothers.

Elderly home alone
Help keep them safe
We can talk on the phone.

There's crises a plenty
Experiencing
The year, "twenty-twenty."

Holocene Extinction

We are in the midst of a Holocene Extinction.
Poor, wealthy, strong or great, the earth makes no distinction.
Thousands of plants and animals dying off each year;
Man continues living, assuming nothing to fear.

An unprecedented global super predator,
Mother Earth has become Humanity's creditor.
Human beings' impact on the environmental
Is leaving a life deficit that's monumental.

Anthropogenic influences without any stops,
Transmission of diseases through livestock and crops.
Population growth, Industrial Revolution,
What's needed *now* is an altruistic solution.

With human growth, and oceanic devastation,
Habitat destruction and vast deforestation;
All leading to an understanding of exactly how;
We've reached the Holocene event that we're facing now.

An eminent mass extinction, the sixth, maybe more,
The end of life, as we know it, knocking at the door.
But, wait! We continue on, and everything is fine;
For, the corporeal can transform to crystalline.

MEDITATIVE STATE

A sea of green and sky of blue leads me to a peaceful serenity
Allowing a quiet time reflecting on the inner person in me
I imagine sitting on the beach with my feet digging into warm sand,
Sensing a powerful cleansing as water waves upon the changing land.

I listen to the rhythmic sounds of rolling water crashing on the beach.
It's lulling me into a Meditative State almost within my reach
I can see myself floating in the water while looking back to the shore
Becoming one with my surroundings, I have opened a mystical door,

Sensing the all-encompassing waters becoming alive within me
I realize just how very small I am in this vital force called the sea,
Thinking of how it all began with a perfectly-planned earthly design
And the stewardship required to care for this land that is now yours and mine.

Many people fight to save our earth, seeking to change man's destructive ways
So that our children's children enjoy this earth in the coming of the days.
My imagined voyage comes to an end upon this discerning sea of green
Bringing new hope for a better world that is ordered, balanced and serene.

MOTHER EARTH

Gentle living earth that we are connected to
Dueling with the damages caused by me and you.
Earth's heart beats laboriously beneath her crust
Calloused mortals say we're just doing what we must.

Are we Earth's guardians who, inertly selfish,
Just keep using whatever whenever we wish?
Or can we open our eyes, becoming aware,
And to our children's childen's generation be fair.

Everything in Balance

Violence and love: Life's a balance of both.
Destruction fertilizes new growth
Love's nurturing spirit breeds beauty
Producing
Timeless Growth
Seeking balance

All things working together to survive,
The very act of being alive,
Too much or too little doesn't work
Equaling
One Stillness
Finding balance

Everything must balance now and again
Forces of water, earth, fire and wind
Thrive together in equilibrium
Co-sharing
The Life Force
Living balance

CINDY: In my younger years, I seemed to live the deep physical and spiritual wounds I had received while growing up over and over, always needing to be rescued or "fixed," which was never enough! It took me realizing I'd imprisoned myself in my own mind, and I was the one causing that everlasting pain. I was actually addicted to the pain and sorrow! Finally, the realization that I no longer needed to be a victim emerged, and I was able to change my attitudes and begin to glean spiritual lessons from these past experiences.

This journey began by asking forgiveness from anyone to whom I may have caused pain, forgiving myself for causing that pain, and forgiving others who had caused me pain. I also had to forgive my "needy" self. Finally, now at peace, I began to grow exponentially, expanding the joy in my life.

SPIRITUAL HEALING

Sadness has overcome me now
In need of a Spiritual Healing
Feeling my strength slowly weaken
Overwhelmed with all that I'm feeling.
Confusing moments come and go
Most problems usually work themselves out.
I might find a lesson or two,
Maybe three, I need to learn about.

After reflective soul searching
Trying to understanding what's inside,
I then meditate on my thoughts
Or in a wise trusted friend I confide.
Easing my mood and allowing
Renewed spirit to soar to great heights,
This brings me just one step closer
To perfecting my soul with deep insights.

CONSCIOUSNESS SHIFT

Reality's illusion is crumbling
right before our eyes
The veil is thinning with Humanity's
agonizing cries.

Vigor is being drained from the current
inhabiting force
Rising to a higher vibrational
and pre-ordained course.

Erupting emotions fill mankind with
anticipation
Magic answers being petitioned in
vain contemplation.

Our inner world is now awakening
right down at the core
For the rhythmic beating heart of misused
Earth can take no more.

Current inhabitants riding on this
living space vessel
Pay homage to self-serving prophecies
with which we wrestle.

And so, the time has come for a higher
world consciousness shift
Or, it's time to let go and start again,
Earth souls set adrift.

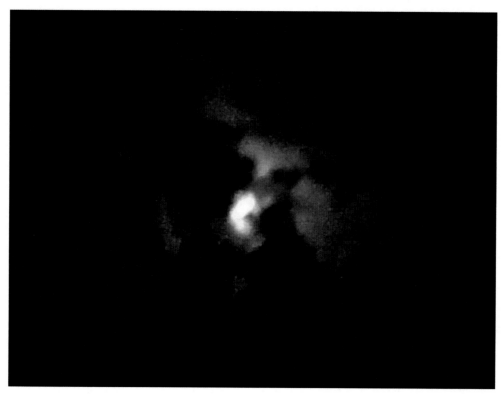

Photo by Alex Bennet

JOURNEY'S DONE

Biding, waiting to fly free
Seeking, searching all that's me
Setting sunlight fades the day
Rising moon-glow lights the way.

Spinning, moving pinpoint light
Flying closer, just in sight
Blazing brighter than the sun
No more bindings: Journey's Done.

VI. Flying Free

KNOWING

Starting out as an emerging inspired spark
A fresh journey begins on which to embark
Finding the discernment that's needed and sought
Growing from a small seed to creative thought.

Sprouting branches, guided speculation
Bring veiled understanding and jubilation
Virgin insights from creative thought flowing
Find me flourishing in a place called knowing.

CINDY: I've been through what seems like many lifetimes in my life. So many memories, and I'm not sure if I have enough time to write them all down. Some of my adventures I would like to experience again, but some of them were just lessons I needed to learn. I've naively walked into places and situations that I should never have been. I'm positive that someone or something was constantly watching over me, maybe even angels. All the good times and all the missed directions, there was always a hand reaching out willing to help as I slowly opened my blind eyes.

It took a good majority of my life to learn that love was not something I had to look for and find in another, but that love was already all around me in everything on this earth, and it cannot be possessed or earned. When I learned that love is the source that holds this whole world together, I began to understand that this earth is a testing ground to learn the lessons we need to get us all ready for the Love we came from and the Love we are returning to.

Awakening

Opening eyes are beginning to see
What was always right in front of me
Took a long time, this learning how
Had to look past the here and now.

.

Awareness explodes in my brain
All the demons are now restrained
If not for God, this would not be
I've been released, and I am free!

CINDY: I've had to forgive myself for my naivety and mistakes, and for going through life with blinders on. I regret that I could have lived more in the present instead of wasting so much precious time as a victim in survival mode. That said, I'm thankful that I no longer feel like a victim, and only hope that anyone I may have caused pain by my fear, naivety or ignorance can forgive me.

All the loneliness I felt growing up and as a young adult has more than healed as I've learned true love by experiencing it abundantly with my five beautiful children and the wonderful people who have come in and out of my life. I'm so thankful for these special spirits.

It is my hope that my children, and their children and on through the generations, will learn these lessons much faster than I did, not carrying forward the generational demons residing within every cell of our bodies through DNA. My simple advice is: *Take care of your minds and bodies, learn spiritual truths, and be at peace with yourself and those around you.*

CONSCIOUSNESS RISING

Awakening to the world
Awareness of who you are
Conscious of life around you

Learning how to love others
Sharing our lives together
Balancing the emotions

Knowing the earth also lives
Seeing what needs to be done
Making a greater difference

Looking inward to the soul
Clearing away all the weeds
Maturing in the spirit

Giving back to those in need
Preparing for the journey
Returning to the presence

Embracing Life!

HEAR THE CHIMES

I so need to hear the chimes
Ringing once again,
Bringing to my worn, tired mind
A peace from within.

As a gentle rolling breeze
Conveys a chime's tune,
I'm yearning to hear again
The bright music soon.

Reminiscing the feelings
Those ringing chimes brought,
Enter peaceful spirit with
Clarity of thought.

Needing to engage in a
Meditative quest,
The chiming music lulls me
Into blessed rest.

HUMMINGBIRD

One morning I was taking a nap on the garden swing
When I perceived what felt much like a stare.
Opening my eyes, looking at me was a Hummingbird
That seemed to be suspended in the air.
His eyes locked on mine, I could almost reach out and touch him
On this beautiful and warm sunny day.
He appeared very still, while his wings beat extremely fast
Both his sides were a moving blur of grey.

It felt like this Hummingbird had something to say to me
And he did not show the least bit of fear
We fixated at one another for a few moments
It was just unbelievably surreal
I wanted to stay captured in the moment for awhile
But alas, it was just not meant to be.
His body moved away from me, a little to the left,
Then one more time he looked back towards me.

I understood that he was a friendly little creature
And he had something he wanted to share
I wondered, was he as curious of me as I him
As he hung there suspended in the air?
I gently reached out to touch this beautiful little bird
Before he'd fly away from me to hide
In a split second he moved away with a whirling noise
Which left me feeling so empty inside.

I have often looked back and thought about that Hummingbird
It all appeared so magical back then.
There's an extremely clear picture of that bird in my mind,
Watching it happen again and again.
Just why did he stop to visit with me on his journey
Gathering nectar on that sunny day?
I can only hope someday it will become clear to me
What that little Hummingbird had to say.

BIG DADDY CHAIR BEAR

There was a Daddy Bear with money to spare
Who wanted to buy a new Daddy Bear chair.
Consulting with home designer, Momma Bear,
Making the furniture match was her only care.

So, Daddy and Aussie Bear went to the store
Found a nice chair he thought his wife would adore.
Drove it home, and had to push it through the garage door.
It did match, but was huge and hard to ignore.

"Where shall we put this?" Momma Bear did implore
"Put Mom's chair in the corner" he said with a roar,
"And mine right here in the middle of the floor."
And thought to himself, what a fantastic score.

"My Ohio state blanket fits the back of the chair.
Look, the chair's big enough for two bears to share!"
Mom wants to say it's ugly, but didn't dare,
After all, he'd become the Big Daddy Chair Bear.

CINDY: This verse was inspired by my youngest daughter. And, in the mode of "the rest of the story", eventually, over time, that chair was relegated first to a corner, and then to the garage, disappearing when the appropriate circumstances made it possible.

So often it is the little things in life that stick in the front of our minds … but, then, maybe that's my OCD talking! LOT's of little things stick in the front of my mind!

Intuitive thinking
And imagination
Reaching toward heaven
Meditatively find
Etheric state of Mind.

Photo by Kathy Carlisle

MEDITATIVE HOME

Let me take you to a peaceful place in my mind, where I go to get away from this life race. A safe and comfortable inner world called by the name, "My Place". The house sits off the ground on stilts, high enough that anyone could sit under. Water flows like a brook beneath the house which comes with heavy rains and thunder.

A home made of bamboo, and wicker, with throw rugs on the wooden floors. The walls are filled with shuttered windows and all four sides of the house have doors. My feet feel finely finished bamboo floors as I walk out onto the porch. All the screened decks surround the house, and both sides of every door have a torch.

The veranda supports aged wicker benches for sitting and resting at the end of day. There are soft cushions and blankets for warmth with throw pillows where your head can lay. A gentle breeze catches soothing sounds from many different kinds of hanging chimes. When you walk down the stairs, surrounding the home, there are trees including oranges and limes.

The bedroom contains lots of blankets on an enticing, comfy bed. Pulling the comforter up to my neck, the fluffy pillows welcome my head. I drift off to sleep listening to cricket songs floating through the cool night, dreaming of the warm distant beach waiting for me in the morning sunlight.

Waking up to morning song birds with a breeze rustling through the leaves, daybreak peers through the darkened shadows of the fading nighttime trees. Bare feet gliding down the wood stairs, reaching the soft grassy land, following the forest path till at last, the path opens to the ocean sand.

Coming out of the sheltered forest during this tranquil morning sunrise hour, the sounds of waves fill my senses with the ocean's overwhelming power. Digging my feet into the warm sand, with the sea breeze gently cooling me, I sit watching the perfect sunrise while sipping on my hot herbal tea.

Heading back, my thoughts shift and focus on likely visitors expected this day. I gather fruit and chamomile for tea in hopes that new and old friends might stay. What a wonderful place for one to come for a much-needed rejuvenation. I could forever stay in this meditative home, embracing a permanent vacation!

A peaceful dwelling.

HAND IN HAND

Hand in hand we walked through life
Living a collective dream
Sometimes a roaring river
Other times a gentle stream.

Standing by one another
Through trials and tribulations
Growing, learning and giving
Spawning combined creations.

Slowly our youthful vigor
Diminished through the years,
With days of joyous laughter
And sometimes sadness and tears.

Through elations and struggles,
Whether arduous or fun,
We will forever remain
Hand in hand, 'til life is done.

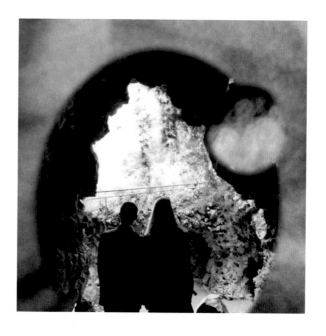

Precious Moments

Every moment in life is so precious
Like when experiencing physical love
Time that cannot ever be recaptured
Becomes just a faded memory thereof.

Now those reflections from a time long past
Seem like a futile power struggle game,
A choreographed dance daily improvised
With which carnal passions tried to be tame.

Now seeking love on a higher level
And not driven by sensuous desires,
I'm drawn towards agape affinity,
Quenching the flesh with truth's spiritual fires.

AVATAR

If I could create an avatar for myself
I'd so wish to be invisible
Seeing only good residing in each other,
For love makes existence livable.

I would cross the oceans, and climb mighty mountains
Embracing life changes within me,
Cleansing the heart of long-avoided skeletons
Interfering with what other's see.

I would soar above the breathing river of life
And fly down to help someone in need,
Embracing the surrounding dynamic life force
While nurturing every single soul seed.

What more could we ask from this earthbound existence
Then sharing life lessons that we learn,
Reflecting on this planet's copious bounty
Which is given for us to discern.

This unfolding coursework will soon be behind us
Just be sure you've expressed your voice.
We can wallow in pain or revel in beauty,
Self-absorbed or selfless… It's your choice

GLIMPSES OF

A parent holding a new born child
In a loving, caring arm.
Stopping to help a hurt animal,
Rendering it safe from harm.

Caring for someone you do not know,
From which you lovingly learn
To give to others without asking
For anything in return.

Helping others without them knowing
When sewing some new life seeds,
Doing what is best for everyone
Sometimes ignoring *your* needs.

Praying for someone that needs your prayers
Seeking not your glory known
Wisely giving as you live your life
Without showing seeds you've sown.

UNCONDITIONAL LOVE

When doing for others, not keeping score
Just doing for doing's sake
And holding back the "I told you so"
When others make a mistake.

Reaching out with a calm helping hand
Whenever someone may fall
Understanding that the universe
Owes one's self nothing at all.

Have patience when others are learning
However slow and steady
Knowing that others will seek the truth
In time, when they are ready.

Think about the world all around us
And everything that we do.
There're Glimpses of Unconditional Love
Growing within me and you.

SENIOR MOMENTS

Decline in our thinking comes
With physical age,
And getting old slows us down
On this life's grand stage.

The brain is crammed full and it's
Not hard to conceive,
The information that's needed
Is hard to retrieve.

A senior goes to a room
To obtain something,
Then asks, "Why am I in here?"
Not remembering.

It's not a memory problem,
So proclaims the wise.
It's nature's way for seniors
To get exercise.

As a senior, I have learned
Not to live in fear.
There's little fear when you've lived
To be old, my dear.

Now, when people are aging
It's harder to hear.
When the brain's full, there's pressure
On the inner ear.

As I have explained to you
So well and as such,
The brain definitely slows down
From knowing so much!

KNOWLEDGE *to* KNOWING

Eyes look beyond images seeing
Deep within the spiritual being.
Listening past the audible hearing
As outside chatter begins clearing.

Move beyond emotions with feelings
Above the river of life's dealings.
Look beyond appearances showing
Arrival innate knowledge, knowing.

Aperture to the Soul

Looking deep into the eyes
Seeing light beyond the face
Immersed in the sea of life
Connecting to the human race.

Oh! responsive persona
Gazing into what is true
Finding reflective wisdom
lPerceiving the life force in you.

A BUTTERFLY

Wrapped in a secure cocoon and it's getting so tight
Shedding, then waiting for emergence into light,
Searching, scratching, gnawing to find any way out
Contemplating what this earthly cocoon's all about.

When will the life force in this aging body break free
From its wrappings, clinging snugly to this world tree?
Earth-born spirit caught in this struggling vessel of flesh,
What will emerge from this used body when I'm at rest?

Have I finished with what my spirit was sent here for?
Did my life experiences open the right door?
Can the butterfly evolve, and with God commune
While this soul is wrapped in a corporeal cocoon?

GOLDEN CONSCIOUSNESS

Away from all of the world's confusing refashion,
Allow us to bask in love's essential compassion
So, our spirits may soar, using ethereal wings,
And we may see the beauty that life on Earth brings.

As we are moving to a higher dispensation
All life on this planet, including every nation,
United in thought away from lasciviousness
Moving life on earth to a Golden Consciousness.

What lies ahead of us is not a physical fight
People must learn to distinguish darkness from the light.
As minds and bodies move into a divergent state
Together, the darkness we can illuminate!

Look for the light in life
And in others.

INCLUESSENCE

A state of being far beyond
That which one can dream
Unlike anything to this day,
That's ever been seen
Believed to be the very highest
Grand level of change
Covering an unimaginable
And uncharted range!

Living, learning outside the box
Allows us to see
The way corporeals become
All that they can be.
Tapping into the soul self with
An intuitional wing,
Getting glimpses of the essence
That is everything!

CINDY: "Incluessence" is a word conceived and visualized by Jo Dunning. I felt a deep connection to the meaning and meditated on understanding its concept. This is my personal learning about and expression of the word. I'm eternally grateful for Jo Dunning's teachings and eternal ministry.

There are people born into this world with qualities of goodness who serve as examples for all of us. Jo Dunning is such a person, as was Mother Teresa.

Photo by Alex Bennet

Growth

Soul touch

Love so deep

Giving so great

Compassion so vast

Selflessness so complete

Immersed in the light of truth

II. The Eternal Soul and Me

QUANTUM INTELLIGENCE FIELD

All that you will ever know
And all that you will ever be
Is in the Akashic field
For the intuitive to see.

From the very beginning
With every living entity
Accumulated knowledge
Becoming our identity

Beyond the physical world
The prophets and visionaries
Gain cosmic intelligence
Becoming great luminaries.

Through evolved meditation
The quiet peaceful mind can yield
A transcendent consciousness,
A Quantum Intelligence Field.

CINDY: Pondering and gleaning and engrossed in spiritual lessons while being imprisoned in this body of flesh and blood, the eternal soul or essence of a person grows, hopefully, steadily through life. This entity or embodiment of our soul needs continuous seeding and nourishment in order to sustain a balance of steady growth. Without this growth we cannot reach our full potential. And so, we naturally connect with the larger field, and our knowing opens and expands.

LOVE SOUL CONNECTION

Perceiving a glow about the face
Reaching outward with imparted grace
Teaching with chosen conscious action
Exuding loving warm compassion

Listening with a heart of silence
Open to and receiving guidance

Feeling the pulse of humanity
Giving forward and acting selflessly
Hungering for agape perfection
Opening up the love soul connection

BEAUTY

Oh, beautiful soul, love transcending
Feel freedom's truth ascending
Thought, feelings, actions take hold
Beaming beauty from within, behold.

FAMILIAR HOME

A dream, traveling back in time, reoccurred
Though structured, the symbolism was inferred
A Familiar Home that put my soul at rest
A remembering place where I'm not a guest.

Lucid dreamer in a safe inviting place
Known souls welcoming with a loving embrace
Perceiving a home, comfortable and secure,
Though exactly just who I'm with is unsure.

A house of many rooms sharing days of ole
Grounded, talking to an intimate old soul
Feeling I belong here, I don't want to leave
Could I really live here? I so want to believe.

Visiting there for what seemed like a season
Why must I leave? Can you give me a reason?
"I want to stay here," said out loud, with my voice.
I sense unspoken words: "Stay or go, it's your choice."

Lucid dreamer waking from a slumber deep
Finding the way back from a seductive sleep
Leaving the dream open for a discerning
My efforts weren't futile; I'll be returning.

CREATION CODE

Within the flesh is the key
How Creation came to be
The answer is there to find
In every cell of humankind.

The spoken word brought the light
From the void of eternal night
Alpha source shall soon unfold
Hidden in the DNA code.

TIME TRAVELER

Life maneuvers me onward through time
Until this journey is done,
A pendulum swinging to and fro,
One construct to the next one.

There's a yearning inside each of us
To find out where we came from,
Ushering in an awakening,
"A knowing of what's to come."

The time that has gone and is to come
Becomes eventually one.
All life's lessons connect together
When our education's done.

CINDY: One day my sister Alex shared a lucid dream about her beloved friend, partner and husband, David. She was sitting in a lecture room, near the center about four rows back. Beside her sat David's beloved daughter, who had transitioned several years earlier. "It's alright to cry," the daughter said softly to Alex.

So many people … the room was full … and they were all different ages, colors and sizes, softly whispering one to the other, somehow connected. And then, each one, one by one, turned to look up at Alex, and gradually, in a continual wave of faces, the achievements of David were shared. From this sharing, the verse "As the fire dims …" was voiced.

As the fire dims …

As the lucid fire dims, the bright embers still glow.
An accounting is taken of this past stage show.
Untold paths illumined by this soldier's light
Gleaning, gaining, growing from a life of insight.

When each questing soul touched in turn lights up one more
Continued effect, unimaginable score.
Know that this light warrior has sharing left to do
In the dispensation that is just out of view.

DIVINE INSTRUCTOR

Spirit Thought Adjuster touch me
Open my eyes so truth I see
Yielding through choice, I acquiesce
Lift up my soul so I may progress.

Reaching hands surrendered and meek
It's a veiled promise I now seek
Enter into the mind of thought
Oh, indwelling one forever sought.

Flow gently through and intertwine
Perfect my actions, heart and mind
This somatic bound conductor
Listens for the Divine Instructor.

The Myst at Mountain Quest Institute

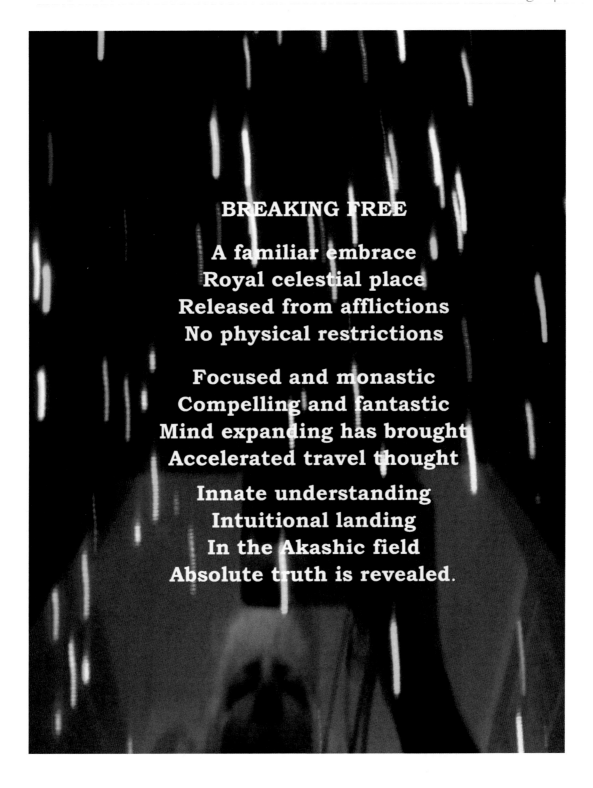

BREAKING FREE

A familiar embrace
Royal celestial place
Released from afflictions
No physical restrictions

Focused and monastic
Compelling and fantastic
Mind expanding has brought
Accelerated travel thought

Innate understanding
Intuitional landing
In the Akashic field
Absolute truth is revealed.

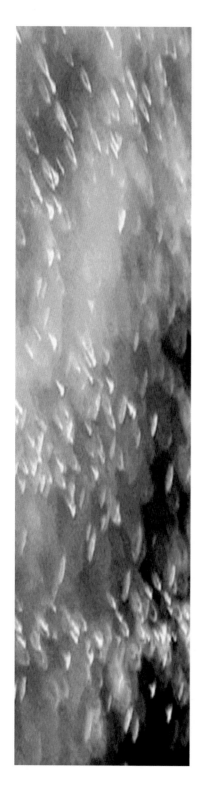

GREAT KNOWING

This well-used and worn-out vessel
That is failing me now
Is piloted by my spirit
Still sailing this ship, somehow
When feeling like I cannot climb
Not even one more rung
In comes innate inspiration,
And a journey has begun.

Clouds separate, bringing focus
Intense clarity comes.
My free spirit rhythmically moves
To a different set of drums
Then guided through the regions of
A now expanding mind,
Opening great knowing beyond
The unbarred illumined blind.

Painting pictures with words of what
The mind's eye can now see,
A divine and peaceful place where
I can feel completely free.
My inspiring journey then ends,
Releasing the deep thought.
I've received the inspiration
And awareness that I sought!

WATCHING OVER YOU

Drawing by Amanda Insogna

My grandchild came to me as if looking for an answer he could not find
His face looked really worried, with something enormous on his mind
He stands up tall right in front of me, and intently looks into my eye,
"Grandma, you are old" he says, then asks "Are you soon going to die?"

Gently I spoke, "Being born and dying happens to all, my little one.
You have many years ahead of you, and yes, mine are almost done."
I could see the concern in his eyes, and wondered what should I say or do?
I ask, "When I die, can I be an angel watching over you?"

"Yes", he answers calmly, seemingly just fine with our talk about death.
I said, "I would love to watch over you when I breathe my last breath."
Then, putting my arms around him, we hug and kiss good night.
I watch him walk away, knowing everything will be all right.

JOURNEY OF THE SOUL

Human experience
A lifetime of growth slowly rising
Acting, reacting and synthesizing.

Spirit persona
New experiences remanning
Being, reflecting and conscious planning.

Divine quintessence
Peering through prisms, bending the light
Giving a full spectrum to inward sight.

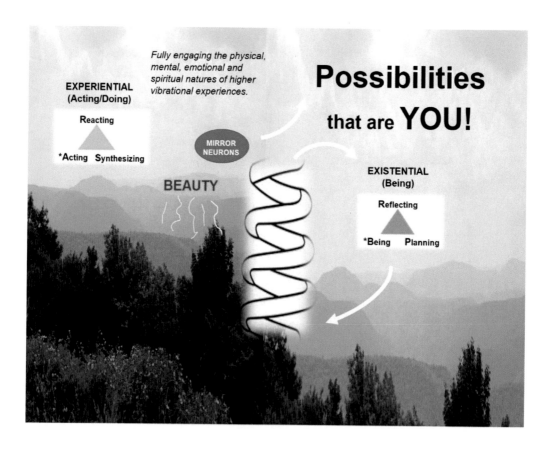

CINDY: And, finally, I ask the questions I have spent my life trying to answer, and there are, from this aged but limited frame of reference, answers that emerge. While Life is a very personal journey, I offer these answers for your consideration and exploration.

LIFE QUESTIONS

Who am I?
Soul intervention
Sum of many lessons learned
And experiences discerned
Through a Guided Divine Intention.

Where did I come from?
Looking for life's source,
A rhythmical vibrating
Forever resonating
Firmament singularity force.

So, Why am I here?
Love resurrected
Unchained hearts' subjection
Finding beauty's reflection
Man's inner adversity perfected.

Where am I going?
Death's door brings new sight
With a lifetime reviewing
Cleansing the soul, renewing
Thereupon, returning to the light.

EVOLUTION

Intertwined in the spiral birth
Animated on living earth
One Creation
One vibration
Concatenated and diverse
Connecting to the Universe.

Consciousness drives the illusions
Seemingly random infusions
Constant changing
Rearranging
Awakening inner seeings
Cultivating evolved beings.

CINDY: Now that I'm coming to the end of my lifespan, at least it feels that way, the body is mostly controlled by the Parkinson's Disease. With all the stiffening and aching, I cannot override the pain as easily as I used to, but there are still times when I can rise above my affliction … I soar in the clouds during those all too short but astounding moments in time. I am thankful for whatever is left, and will continue on, seeking and growing until my time here is done … There is so much wonderment left for me still to discover, or maybe even new or fresh beginnings. It's been a miraculous and phenomenal journey!!!!!

FINISH LINE

There are many roads going in all directions
Taken by a multitude of people and creeds
Altogether we are one, learning and growing
From spiritually planted inner soul seeds.

　　We don't really know when our journeys are finished
　　With our delusional perception of Earth time
　　Just try to stay focused on the lesson at hand
　　Keeping an open mind's eye on the finish line.

GENTLY ENTER INTO THE LIGHT

Old and tattered body worn
From this earthly life soon torn
Waiting for love's tender guide
Leading souls to the other side.

Though leaving loved ones behind
Those gone before soon you'll find
No more pain and no more fight
"Gently Enter into The Light".

CHANGE

All life transforms
Nothing stands still
We're born to grow
As our spirits fill.

Building it up
Growth evolving
Tearing it down
Till death's resolving.

WISDOM

C auses of life pain answered
A ccidents with their reasons
M istakes with their corrections
E vents gone wrong and solved.

May your life be full of love and learning.

THE ETERNEL SOUL AND ME

The eternal soul co-mingling in me
Peering into the deep, wanting to see
Meandering through valleys and over hills
Following paths fraught with stumbles and spills
Pondering teachings, often feeling inept
For me some were difficult to accept

As each passage before me would unfold
Connecting me with my eternal soul
Listening and growing with each life trial
I was slowly expanding all the while
A union of soul and body power
Blossoming every blooming life flower

-Cindy Lee Scott

Postlude: All Becomes One Becomes All

Journey through my lives of what came before,
Reaching far back to see my reflections.
Musty flowers fill the air about me
Flooding my senses from all directions.

Floating and weaving and drifting through time
As a familiar fragrance fills the air.
Focused, still wondering where I came from,
Going further back through time if I dare.

Lanky personage in a dreamlike state
Above a lifeless planet, just drifting.
Light violet face with metallic-like suit;
Turning of day to darkness is shifting.

Splitting cracks tear the metallic body,
Streaming out a bright pulsating white light.
All is escaping that's contained within
Under the night sky, with tiny stars bright.

Body floating within the atmosphere
While the light from within escapes its wall.
All beings contained in the light are one;
In the radiance I 'm one with the all.

Coming back with many faces showing,
All nationalities, cradle to tomb,
Trailing quickly across the universe
Entering back in, through my mother's womb.

Arriving back to the place I began,
And meditating on what I recall,
A guided impartation entered in:
"The all will be one and one will be all."

INDEX BY TITLE

INDEX BY FIRST LINE

Rising Consciousness through Disruption and Corruption:

An Uplifting Journey of Verse

by Cindy Lee Scott

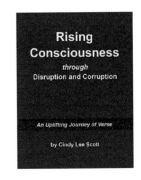

Cindy begins her introduction: "I am not al person who is particularly drawn to politics." However, she was deeply troubled by the incision-division that was continuing to create a widening gulf between the people of the United States. This collection of prose and poetry motifs represent Cindy's journey searching for truth and, ultimately, discovering the beauty that can be found in change, not only politically but inwardly. And ultimately, she recognized that this is a great time of accelerated growth for humans, and, somehow, we must come together to raise our consciousness as a whole. Available in softback from Amazon.com

Also available from MQIPress: The *Myst* Series

The Journey into the Myst ... A true story of the Paranormal (Volume I)

Patterns in the Myst: Messages from the Universe (Volume II)

The Heart, the Mind and the Myst: A Neuronal Dance with the Universe (Volume III)

"What we are about to tell you would have been quite unbelievable to me before this journey began. It is not a story of the reality either of us has known for well over our 60 and 70 years of age, but rather, the reality of dreams and fairytales." This is the true story of a sequence of events that happened at Mountain Quest, situated in a high valley of the Allegheny Mountains of West Virginia. **The story begins with a miracle**, expanding into the capture and cataloging of thousands of pictures of electromagnetic spheres widely known as "orbs." **This joyous experience became an exploration into the unknown** with the emergence of what the author's fondly call the *Myst*, the forming and shaping of non-random patterns such as human faces, angels and animals. As this phenomenon unfolds, you will discover how the Drs.Alex and David Bennet began to observe and interact with the *Myst*. Volumes I and II available in Kindle and softback from Amazon.com

See MQIPress Conscious Look Books!

The Possibilities that are YOU!

by Alex Bennet

All Things in Balance
The Art of Thought Adjusting
Associative Patterning and Attracting
Beyond Action
Connections as Patterns
Conscious Compassion
The Creative Leap
The Emerging Self
The Emoting Guidance System
Engaging Forces
The ERC's of Intuition
Grounding
The Humanness of Humility
Intention and Attention
Knowing
The Living Virtues of Today
Me as Co-Creator
Seeking Wisdom
Staying on the Path
Transcendent Beauty
Truth in Context

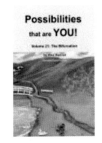

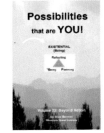

Also,

The Intelligent Social Change Journey
by Alex Bennet, David Bennet, Arthur Shelley, Theresa Bullard and John Lewis
(Available in soft back on amazon.com)

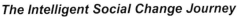

Made in the USA
Monee, IL
18 February 2021

59721013R00112